Paul The Theologian

GOD'S WORD TODAY VIII

A New Study Guide to the Bible

Emil A. Wcela

Paul the Theologian

*His Teaching
in the Letter to the Romans*

*Suggestions for Reflections
by Sr. Jeanne Monahan O.P.*

PUEBLO PUBLISHING COMPANY

NEW YORK

Nihil Obstat: *Daniel V. Flynn, J.C.D.*
               Censor Librorum

Imprimatur: ✠ *James P. Mahoney, D.D.*
               Vicar General,
               Archdiocese of New York

Design: Frank Kacmarcik, D.F.A.

CONTENTS

PREFACE

Interest in the Scriptures continues to grow. Men and women
individually and in groups read, reflect on, discuss, pray from
the Bible. I have taught, led, participated in such groups.
This participation has convinced me that, despite all the
worthwhile material on the Bible already available, there
are still gaps to be filled for those people who truly care
about the Bible but have had little or no preparation to
extract its riches.

Several excellent guides to the Bible exist in the format of
booklet series in which each volume provides commentary
and explanation on a separate book of the Bible. However,
for someone becoming acquainted with the Bible, to work
through each book one by one can be a formidable task.

Other books focus on themes and main ideas distilled from
the whole Bible. As valuable as such theologies and over-
all views are, there is still a need for a familiarity with the
text of the Bible itself.

In this series, substantial portions of the Scriptures—extensive
enough to convey style, language, tone—are the indispensable
starting point. Essential background and explanation are
provided and the lasting import of the text is suggested.
Possibilities for individual or group reflection are offered.

When the reader has completed this series, he will have
encountered many themes and main ideas, and this through
a selected and guided reading of the text itself. This over-
all view can be filled in by further study of the individual
books of the Bible.

The general plan emerges from a listing of the titles in this
series. It is my strong recommendation that anyone using
the series begin with Volume I. If the principles presented
there are grasped, the spadework will be done for understanding what follows.

"Indeed, God's word is living and effective, sharper than
any two-edged sword. It penetrates and divides soul and
spirit, joints and marrow; it judges the reflections and
thoughts of the heart" (Hebrews 4.12).

INTRODUCTION

PAUL AND ROME

This volume is meant to follow up *Paul the Pastor*. When one tries to study and reflect on Paul and his presentation of God, Jesus, and the Christian life, two letters serve as very full and enlightening overviews.

The First Letter to the Corinthians shows Paul in his role as pastor. A young and lively community experiences growing pains. Questions about theology, about morality, about day-to-day living arise. Paul, the founder of the church at Corinth, responds to the questions, gives direction and encouragement, recalls basic Christian teaching, slaps a wrist here and there.

Paul is not simply an answer machine. He speaks from his own knowledge of the Christian faith and from traditions that he shares with others. He speaks from his own religious experience and the life in Jesus that was his.

The Letter to the Corinthians is a somewhat disjointed and miscellaneous product. It is rich with insights into Christian life and teaching, but the riches are contained in a sometimes explanatory, sometimes commanding, sometimes patient, sometimes indignant, but always loving letter. The letter moves in fits and starts in different directions as Paul responds to the issues raised by the reports and delegation that have reached him from Corinth.

The Letter to the Romans is something different.

A consideration of letter-writing in general, and of Paul's letters in particular, and an account of Paul's life can be found in *Paul the Pastor*.

Here, only the background necessary for understanding the Letter to the Romans will be presented.

THE CHRISTIAN COMMUNITY AT ROME

Paul was not the founder of the Christian community at Rome. In fact, the founder still remains unknown. Since Rome was a focus for travel and trade, early Christian missionaries, or even simple travellers, could have brought there the message of and about Jesus.

Paul seems to have little specific information about the church at Rome. Some bits of information had probably been brought to him by Priscilla and Aquila, who had been converted from Judaism to Christianity, very likely at Rome. The Roman authorities had driven them and others from Rome as the result of some sort of religious conflict, possibly between Jews and Christians of Jewish background. Paul lived with Priscilla and Aquila during his stay in Corinth.

Most of the Christians there were of non-Jewish background and belonged to the poorer, even slave, elements of society.

WHY A LETTER TO THE ROMANS?

Please read: Romans 15.14-33

Paul informs the Roman Christians of his plans.

The year is 57 or 58. Paul is still at Corinth. He intends to return to Jerusalem. He has been encouraging the groups of Christians in the cities and towns of Asia Minor and Greece to take up a collection. The money received is to benefit the Christians in Jerusalem who are facing hard times.

Basic Christian charity, concern for those suffering or less fortunate, is an obvious motive. But Paul sees beyond this. At a time when relations between Christians of Jewish background and those of Gentile background are strained, Paul sees an opportunity for building bridges between the two groups. The collections will be a living and concrete sign of the unity among Christians. Members of the non-Jewish churches of Greece and Asia Minor are willing to contribute to the needs of their broth-

ers and sisters of Jewish background. And Paul, the apostle
to the Gentiles, by bringing the collection to Jerusalem himself,
will show the strength of the cords of faith that bind together
all those who have accepted the message of Jesus, no matter
what their background.

After Jerusalem, Paul has his sights set on new lands to which
he feels compelled to bring the Gospel. He intends to travel to
Spain, the outer western limit of the civilized world as it was
then known. On the way to Spain, Paul would do the most
natural thing in the world. He would stop in Rome, the heart
of the all-pervasive Roman Empire.

A DIFFERENT KIND OF LETTER

The Letter to the Romans is different from the First Letter to
the Corinthians and the other letters Paul wrote. He had never
met most of the Roman Christians. He did not know the details
of the life of the church there.

Furthermore, the letter does not seem to be addressed to specific problems or situations, as Paul's other letters are. It reads
more like a general statement of the basic human situation and
how Jesus fits into it.

Because of these peculiarities of the Letter to the Romans,
scholars cannot agree on why it was written. Some hold that
since Paul was about to visit a community which did not know
him personally, he sent ahead a kind of letter of introduction
that expressed his basic beliefs. Others claim that if the letter
is read carefully enough, traces can be found of specific issues
and problems to which Paul was speaking. Still others hold
that this letter was in the nature of a general instruction sent
to several different churches. In the course of time, the address,
"To all in Rome," became permanently affixed.

For our purposes, we shall follow the tradition that the letter
was written to Rome. We can leave aside a detailed answer to
the question "Why?"

Romans contains much that appears in other letters, notably the Letter to the Galatians. But here, Paul has time to work out in a quiet, reflective way ideas that were expressed in other letters, sometimes in angry response to errors, sometimes in brief sketches and passing references.

The result is a well-thought out, carefully organized summary of fundamentals.

The letter does not deal with all aspects of Christian teaching, but it deals with what is perhaps the most basic of all questions for anyone who ever calls himself, or herself, "Christian."

What is Jesus Christ all about?

CHAPTER I

THE SURPRISING JUSTICE OF GOD

PAUL, SERVANT AND APOSTLE

Please read: Romans 1.1-7

Paul describes himself to those who read or hear his letter. He is "a servant of Christ Jesus."

To most people around us, servants are an expensive luxury belonging to a bygone age. They glide silently through rambling estates as formal and formidable butlers, as maids and house-keepers dressed in neat black uniforms and starched aprons. Or, in a more familiar situation, servants are the hard-working ladies who come in once a week to clean the house for some-one in the neighborhood who is just a little better off. Even for them, we would never use the word "servant."

Paul got the expression, "servant of Jesus Christ," from his Jewish background. A servant of God was one who believed in God, and who showed this belief in the acts of worship he or she performed and in the upright and noble moral code by which he or she lived. The title could be applied to a single individual and it could also fit the whole people. In a more emphatic way, a "servant of God" was someone whom God had chosen for a special role. Moses and David and other figures in the history of Israel are especially referred to as "servants of God" in the Hebrew Scriptures.

Paul develops this use of the word. By calling himself "a servant of Jesus Christ," he affirms that he belongs totally to Jesus Christ. He does not cringe in fear before the master of his life

1

but he loves him. Paul lives for Jesus and has placed himself at his service. The sign of this service to God and Jesus is Paul's service to others. The special service to which Paul has been called is that of preaching God's word all over the world.

Paul also calls himself an "apostle." The word literally means "one who is sent." For Paul, it has a special significance. An apostle is one to whom the Risen Lord has appeared and given the mission of bringing the Christian message to others.

Paul's letter is all about the Gospel, the "good news." The good news that Paul will proclaim has always been in God's mind and has been working out in human history for many years. It was foretold by the prophets who spoke for God during the centuries of Israel's history.

This good news is all about God's Son who belonged to the family of David. Born of this line of kings, he was a man in every way. He shared the heritage of all men, including suffering and death.

Precisely because he shared to the fullest in the lot of humans, the power of God burst forth in him and his work. This power of God, by which all people knowingly or unknowingly yearn to be touched, is now offered to everyone.

Paul burns to share this wonder with all people, including those at Rome.

As is usual in Paul's letter, the greeting is a pointer to what the letter will be about. The main themes are described, the tone of the letter is set.

THE HEART OF THE GOSPEL

Please read: Romans 1.16-17

In these two verses are words of tremendous significance for Paul and for all who would try to sound the depths of the Christian message. Once again, he witnesses to truths to which he will return in greater detail in the course of the letter.

SALVATION

Salvation. That's what every believer hopes for and speaks of
as the final goal of life. But what exactly does salvation mean?
How does one "get saved"? And what is being saved all about?

What anyone hopes to be saved from depends on what he or
she thinks is wrong.

A person with no food wants to be saved from starvation. A
person who has had a serious heart attack wants to be saved
from a second, fatal one. A wealthy stockbroker wants to be
saved from a plunging market. A happy family wants to be
saved from anything that will destroy its happiness.

In the Old Testament, God is presented as a savior, as one who
saves.

He saves his people from slavery in Egypt.

He saves his people from invading enemy armies.

He saves those who trust in him from sickness and death.

But human enemies come and go and come again in never-ending
cycles. Sickness and death, if escaped once, stand waiting on
the sidelines and inevitably conquer.

For the person who reflects on life in the light of God's revelation, the one evil, the one enemy from which we must at all
costs be saved is Sin—with a capital "S." All the other enemies
can be endured—and conquered—as long as there is ultimate
meaning to life. But Sin is precisely setting up wrong ideals,
directions, models. Sin is hitching one's wagon not to a star
but to an off-course, hopelessly lost, gaudy but fizzling, short-
lived rocket. Sin is loss of meaning. No one clearly sees what
remaining on track toward God brings.

After all, the bad times of life, and death itself, come to all, faithful to God or not. But the believer rests confident that closeness to God remains no matter what goes wrong. Even death cannot come between God and the one he loves. Those who love God through thick and thin come to an indescribably beautiful and perfect union with him forever.

Sin loses sight of this. Sin beckons the human pilgrim down a path which seems pleasant and attractive, but which leads further and further away from the peaceful home for which the pilgrim was searching.

Salvation here and now is deliverance from this kind of blind wandering. It is the light to see true life, the strength to pursue true life, the courage and confidence that come from a sense of purpose that is not deception. All of these are God's gifts to us through Jesus Christ.

THE JUSTICE OF GOD

Paul writes that, "in the gospel is revealed the justice of God."

Justice is a difficult word to use in connection with God.

What do you think of when you hear talk of God being "just"? What is your idea of "God's justice"?

Very likely, there is some connection with God's rewarding good and punishing evil. The general understanding of a just God is that he is someone who is both good and fair. To use figurative language, a just God holds in his hands a scale. On one side of the scale, he puts the good deeds of each human; on the other, the evil. He watches the scale as it sways back and forth. If it tips to the evil side, then the one being judged is to be punished. If it goes over to the good side, then the one whose deeds are being weighed is rewarded.

This may be the common understanding of the words, "just" and "justice." But we must remember that Paul and the words and thoughts he used came from a language and culture different from ours. We have to consider the meaning of the words in that context if we are to understand Paul.

The uses of the word in the Old Testament generally get down to one basic idea.

Being just or being righteous means being faithful to the relationship that exists between God and his people. God has entered a relationship in which he has freely, on his own initiative, said, "I will be God to you. I will be a liberating, saving presence in your life."

To this liberating, saving presence of God, the people are to respond cooperatively, joyfully, enthusiastically. This response involves them not only in a relationship with God, but also with their fellows, to whom God is also related, for whom God is also a saving, liberating presence.

Very often, God's justice will be equivalent to his saving, loving activity.

We can illustrate this from the Old Testament. One of the characteristics of much Hebrew poetry is that the two halves of a line of poetry express the same idea in different words. Thus, when there is question about what one part of a line of poetry means, the other part of the line can offer clarification because it so often says the same thing in different words.

So, in Isaiah 51, 4, the first part of the line: "I will make my justice come speedily," is explained by the second part of the line: "my salvation shall go forth." "Justice" and "salvation" mean the same thing here! Psalm 40, 11 reads:
"Your justice I kept not hidden within my heart;
your faithfulness and your salvation I have spoken of:
I have made no secret of your kindness and your truth in
the vast assembly."

In this poetic piece, "justice," "faithfulness," "salvation," "kindness," "truth," are all treated as having roughly the same meaning.

However, God's justice can also refer to other actions that are called for in a given situation by his relationship to his people. Sometimes this may call for forgiveness, sometimes for judgment against sin.

The main point to keep in mind is that justice is basically a relational word. It expresses the fact that God is what he ought to be in relation to people. When used about people, it expresses their being what they ought to be toward God and toward one another.

The greatest act of God's justice is the life, death and resurrection of Jesus Christ, his Son. How this is so will emerge during the course of Paul's presentation. For him, it is clear that these are the ultimate and continuing acts of God's justice and the shock waves from these events will be felt so long as there are people who are confused about life's meaning, trapped by superficialities, blinded by sin, kept from reaching higher by the weight of evil in the world.

There is another very important word in these few verses which sum up what Paul will be writing about in this letter. That word is "faith." We will leave a discussion of the meaning of faith until later.

For now, Paul has let us know that he is going to be talking about the most basic issues of all. He will talk about that reality of God which mankind experiences most deeply. He will talk about what people can and should expect from God. He will talk about the proper response to God. He will talk about the place of Jesus Christ in the scheme of salvation.

SUGGESTIONS FOR REFLECTION

1. In the American culture "servant" implies some lack of equality, a lesser position to that of the one being served. Yet we use the same term in a more favorable context when we speak of a "civil servant," a "public servant," "servant of the servants of God." Would you consider being called "servant" an insult or a compliment? Why? Explain to someone how Paul used the word "servant," both in his relationship to Jesus, and in his relationship to others.

2. Paul saw himself as called to the "special service . . . of preaching God's word all over the world." In your own life is there a "special service" to which you have been called?

3. We usually speak of the "Twelve Apostles" as unique because they walked with Jesus and were witnesses to his resurrection. Why, then, can Paul refer to himself as an "apostle," since he was converted after the death of Jesus?

4. Have you ever been "saved" by anyone from anything, or for anything? E.g., has your life been saved, have you been saved from a catastrophe or blunder, have you been saved until the right moment to be sent in to a game or job, have you been saved by the "skin of your teeth"? Try to recall how you felt before, during, and after the saving moment: how you felt about yourself and toward the person who saved you. In verse 16 Paul says the Gospel "is the power of God leading everyone who believes in it to salvation." Do you experience the same kind of feeling (dependence, privilege, gratitude, etc.) when you consider yourself as being saved by the good news of God's word and power?

5. We sometimes think of "sin" as "an offense against the law of God," rather than something from which we need to be saved because it is "blind wandering" off our course or direction from God, a real danger to our true life. Take a moment to recall a sin in your past life which endangered your real life by taking you off the course from God. Who saved you from the danger? How?

6. What does it mean to you to say, "God is just"? Give a synonym for "justice." In this chapter God's justice is described as a liberating, saving presence in your life; a relationship with God and men which is seen in saving, loving activity; forgiveness; true judgment against sin. How does this compare with your previous idea of justice and just persons? What just person in your life reminds you of God's justice?

7. If the justice of God is a quality of relationship, namely, that God is what he should be in relationship to man (a saving God), and if our justice lies in the relationship of being truly God's people toward him and toward one another, what effect should this have on the ways we practice and interpret justice as rewarding good and punishing evil? On the way we deal with other nations and ethnic groups? Does this new idea of justice change any of your previous attitudes?

8. Many people wonder how God can be called "just" when he allowed his Son, Jesus, who is all goodness and without sin, to suffer and die. After reading this chapter what insights could you share to throw light on the problem?

CHAPTER II

WHERE PEOPLE ARE

Paul begins with a sweeping description of all mankind. In his thought categories the human race is divided into Jews and non-Jews or Gentiles.

Paul considers the situation of each of these groups. He writes not from a theological ivory tower, but from his own experience. What has the flow of events in his own time taught him? What has he gathered from his own experiences? Having lived for perhaps fifty years, having been a devout Jew and now a zealous Christian, having traveled through much of the known world, having lived among many different kinds of people, having prayed and reflected on his own religious experience and his religious tradition, what does Paul have to say about where people are?

THE PLIGHT OF THE PAGANS (NON-JEWS OR GENTILES)

Please read: Romans 1.18-32

All people share a common experience. They are part of a universe which is very obviously greater than they.

From what they experience, they ought to recognize something of the One behind that universe. In the enduring life of the universe, the endless life of the One behind it shines forth. In the greatness of the universe, the tremendous power of the One behind it is reflected. This power must belong to One who by life and strength stands over against the weakness and limitations of humans. This power must belong to the kind of being that the English language designates as "God."

We do not have to get involved in the question of whether Paul is saying that man can prove the existence of God by the use of reason alone. What he does stress is that the wonders of creation can lead people to see beyond themselves and it. The wonders of creation ought to move humans to recognize their insufficiency, their incompleteness, that there is "more." This recognition ought to lead to joyful, spontaneous honoring of God.

This did not happen for the pagans. Instead of their being led by the marvels of the universe to soar beyond it to the God responsible for it all, they became trapped in a kind of vicious circle. They saw the creatures of the universe and explained them as the work of various gods. These gods were false because they all had the weaknesses and flaws of men instead of the greatness of a true creator. Rather than man growing to reflect God, the gods looked more and more like man.

Once this happened, a tragic series of disruptions followed.

Once man makes God into his own image and likeness, he has committed the most devastating perversion. He destroys his ability to look to ideals, visions, even judgments, beyond himself. He is his own measure. This is such a twisting of the true state of things that it weakens all other relationships. Dealings with other human beings and use of the non-human world are corrupted.

Because of their failure to acknowledge the kind of God who was in their world but beyond it, the pagans distorted sexual relationships. They were people filled with "maliciousness, greed, ill will, envy, murder, bickering, deceit, craftiness." They gossiped and slandered. They were "insolent, haughty, boastful, ingenious in their wrongdoing and rebellious toward their parents." They were "men without conscience, without loyalty, without affection, without pity."

Paul sees repeated in every man the sin of Adam in Genesis. Adam refused to accept God and God's way. Standing up to God brought not liberty, peace and fulfillment but the deterioration of life with woman and the rebellion of nature, which would now produce its food only at the price of the sweat of Adam's brow.

It is important to emphasize again that both of these pictures of sin are not simply windy, theological ramblings. They are the result of reflection on human experience and an interpretation of that experience.

They both start from a description of the strained, twisted, often hostile relationship between the different creatures of the universe. And what is the reason for these distortions? The answer is, "All relationships are twisted because man, the crown of creation, has distorted his proper relationship with God." People have refused to accept the fact that they depend on a loving God who has made them for life with himself. People have chosen to focus their gaze on the world alone and to find the meaning of life in what it has to offer. They have not let creation raise their vision to the wonder that is beyond and responsible for everything that exists. Because this is so, every-- thing has gotten terribly mixed up.

THE PLIGHT OF THE JEWS

Please read: Romans 2.1-3.20

What now of a different kind of people? What now of those who recognize God, who are willing to see beyond here and now to someone who holds everything together and gives direction to life? What about those who are willing to recognize and honor the "Godness" of God? What about those whose history has been characterized by the honest efforts of many to follow where God would lead? What about the Jews of Paul's days?

It is relatively easy to point to the grosser and more obvious vices of a pagan world. What about those who have moved beyond outright sins and try to achieve a more noble life?

Surprisingly, Paul's view of the people fitting this description, and with whom he has had most contact, is just as distressing. They too are caught by Sin.

The important question is "Why?" What has Paul experienced as defective in those who have claimed to know and live by God's directions?

Paul's insight is that simply knowing the way one ought to live is not, by itself, enough to make one live that way.

God is the judge of all, Jews and Gentiles, and he will "repay every man for what he has done: eternal life to those who strive for glory, honor, and immortality by patiently doing right; wrath and fury to those who selfishly disobey the truth and obey wickedness" (Rom. 2.6-8).

In Paul's day, those who claimed a privileged relationship with God knew that this relationship carried with it a special way of life. They failed to live up to that way of life. "Instructed by the law, you know his will." But, "You who preach against stealing, do you steal? You who forbid adultery, do you commit adultery? . . . You who pride yourself on the law, do you dishonor God by breaking the law? As Scripture says, 'On your account the name of God is held in contempt among the Gentiles' " (Rom. 2.21-24).

The fatal flaw of the Jews was that they did not let their failures in living up to God's way of life lead them to acknowledge their own weakness and so become aware of their total dependence on God.

Religious men of Paul's day had become too sure of themselves. They believed they had God all figured out in their system of rules and regulations. Their basic insights were sound. They truly were recipients of God's revelation. But they had gotten so comfortable in their own understanding of what God wanted that they were blinded to the truth that God could not be imprisoned in their system of understanding. They did not let their moral failings serve as a warning to their complacency, to their certainty that they had all the answers. They were not open to a God who could move into their lives in new and wonderful ways. They could not accept Jesus because he and his message were different, unexpected, not fitting into the game plan they had worked out for God.

THE HUMAN SITUATION

In the broad sweep, Paul has painted a discouraging, a hopeless picture of the situation of mankind as he knew it.

Creation is indeed marvellous and mankind is a glory of creation. All created things, especially mankind, reflect the greatness of God.

At the same time, human destiny depends on the proper relationship with God.

But those who do not know about God through the intimacy of his special self-revelation, those who know him only by his reflection in the works of creation, have a history of blindness which distorts and conceals that reflection.

And those who claim to know God intimately because he has spoken to them reveal by their lives that the intimacy has not had the effect to be expected. Simply knowing God does not mean that one will live out the implications of that knowledge, any more than knowing what honesty or love are all about will make one live honestly or lovingly.

Put bluntly, all mankind seems lost, condemned to wander forever, searching for meaning and truth, and even when that is found, unable to make that meaning and truth work in daily life.

Paul ends this section by hooking together a miscellaneous collection of quotations from the Old Testament. What they have in common is that they each testify in some way to human sinfulness. When woven together, they form an ugly tapestry picturing mankind as guilty and separated from God.

"There is no just man, not even one; . . .
 no one in search of God.
All have taken the wrong course, . . .
  not one of them acts uprightly, no, not one.
  Their mouths are full of curses and bitterness.
Swiftly run their feet to shed blood;
The path of peace is unknown to them;
  the fear of God is not before their eyes" (Rom. 3.10-12, 14-18)

What makes this all somewhat difficult to take is that Paul's description applies not only to the slice of humanity he knew in his day but to all people, always.

Does our experience show us anything different from Paul's? Can we say that we experience only, or even mostly, positive things about the possiblilities of mankind? Can we say that all people at least recognize a life and power beyond their own and live out what this implies—that it is not worth killing and robbing and abusing others just for the sake of this life here and now? Can we say that those who claim closeness to God witness by their lives to the ideals they profess?

SUGGESTIONS FOR REFLECTION

1. "The wonders of creation can lead people to see beyond themselves and it. The wonders of creation ought to move humans to recognize their insufficiency, their incompleteness, that there is 'more.' " How would today's atheists answer this statement? Do Christians today act as though they believe it and live accordingly, or are today's Christians sometimes more like the "pagans" Paul describes? If Christians were to live accordingly today, how might they be recognized?

14

2. The results of sin are shown here through two theological images, namely, that men's relationships with each other and with nature had deteriorated. How does Paul's reflection on human behavior resemble that of the author of Genesis? Do you observe an improvement in these relationships in our times?

3. What attitudes and conditions are required for living in a "privileged relationship with God"? Is it ever possible for a person, even when enjoying a "privileged relationship with God" to live the way of life it demands? What puts Christians in a "privileged relationship with God"?

4. In Paul's experience many religious Jews were certain that they had all the answers, that they understood perfectly what God wanted and how he would act. They presumed on their "special-ness" and thought they could control God and holiness with their systems and regulations. Describe a modern day "saint," a truly religious person, and how that person would express dependence on God. Do you know of any Christian groups that foster or nurture this type of holiness today?

CHAPTER III

WHAT GOD DOES ABOUT THE
HUMAN SITUATION

Please read: Romans 3.21-26

After the opening lines of this letter, Paul went to great lengths
to make clear just what he thought of the situation of each of us.
The picture is a depressing one. Everyone stands weighted
down by the burden of being human. That burden makes it impossible to shake loose from the unfortunate turn for the worse
that the world has taken. That burden makes it impossible to
stand high enough and straight enough to begin to glimpse the
wonder of the God who created the world. Even when God is
seen with some clarity, the burden of sin involved in being human
keeps man from relating to him with love and trust.

As Paul describes it, mankind is pitiable. Men and women are
trapped and made helpless by the created world. The world that
they were intended to rule in peace and harmony has become
their tyrannical master.

God created people free. Now that they have abused that freedom and rebelled against the wisdom and goodness of God, they
are reaping the fruits of their wrong-headed pride.

Fortunately for us, Paul's analysis of the situation, based on his
experience, is not the end of the story but the beginning.

In five verses, Paul describes how God deals with the poor beings
he has created who have so spoiled their own possibilities for
life and happiness.

16

God shows his "justice."

The famous line has it, "To thine own self be true." As we have seen, God is just when he is true to himself. The self to which he is to be true is not an angry, punishing, stern judge but a loving Father who lifts his errant children from the terrible plight into which their wilfulness and failure to trust him have gotten them.

REDEMPTION THROUGH JESUS CHRIST: NOT QUITE UNDERSTOOD

This word, redemption, will either say nothing or say too much to many who read or hear it.

It will say nothing to many Catholics of the younger generation who have not grown up with it as part of their religious vocabulary.

It will probably say too much to an older generation of Catholics. A popular understanding of redemption went like this:

"To redeem" means to buy back. A bracelet left in a pawn shop in time of financial troubles is redeemed by returning to the pawn shop proprietor the money he lent to the hard-pressed owner.

In Greece and Rome, a person taken in war could be redeemed. The captive, unable to help himself, could be ransomed by the payment of a sum of money to his captors by his family and friends.

As the word took on religious meaning, the idea became something like this:

Man had sinned against God. Therefore, he owed something to God. Man had to pay back for what he had done wrong.

But the whole transaction was impossibly uneven. How could

humans possibly pay back God?

Suppose a person destroyed a famous painting worth
$20,000,000. Caught in the act, obviously guilty, the person is
told that he will be set free as soon as he pays back the value of
the picture. But how does one pay off a $20,000,000 debt
when one makes $10,000 a year? That's 2000 years of salary!

Impossible! The culprit is doomed never to be free. What he
must do to make up for his crime is totally beyond his capabil-
ities.

How can anyone make up for a sin, an offense against God? It
is difficult enough to undo the wrong we might do to another
person like ourselves. But how make up with the Infinite, the
All-Perfect, the All-Good God? This is altogether out of the
reach of any human, and even of all humans together.

God, aware of the dilemma of his creatures, did not wish to leave
them forever separated from him, forever guilty. He wished to
make it possible for the debt they owed to be paid. The only
one capable of paying the debt to God was God himself. So the
Son, God himself, became man. That put someone in the world
in the ranks of humans who had the capacity to pay the debt
owed to God. To use our example, the Son become man is
equivalent to a benefactor with $20,000,000 saying, "I know you
can't pay what you owe because you haven't got that kind of
money. But I do have that much money and I will pay for you."
Redemption meant, in this understanding, the payment by Jesus
Christ of a debt unpayable by anyone else. The debt was owed
to God the Father. Jesus' life and death was the payment that
balanced the books, cleaned the slate, between God and man.

REDEMPTION: A BIBLICAL VIEW

If we stay with the way the Bible uses the word redemption as
the act of God, we find ourselves with an important difference
from the understanding summarized above.

18

This difference has to do with the fact that the word does not carry with it the somewhat harsh idea of Jesus Christ having to pay a price for us to God the Father.

The basic meaning of the verb "to redeem" when used in relation to God is simply "to free." God redeems or frees his people from slavery in Egypt, from the captivity in the far-off land of Babylon, from sinful times and a sinful world. There is no payment of a price, no hint of books to be balanced before God can move to help his pathetic people. God simply acts. He frees. He liberates. He redeems.

Lest this seem to be much ado about nothing, it must be pointed out that accepting the biblical notion of redemption rather than the one sketched earlier can do much to clarify our idea of God.

God the Father loses the unfortunate image of strict heavenly accountant. It took some clear thinking to work around the scene of a God saying to himself, "They have really gotten themselves into a mess. I'd like to help them. But look at the account book. They have committed more offenses than I could ever possibly forgive. I will solve that by having my Son become a human. Then he will be able to wipe the debt off the books and I can be nice to them again."

Remove the notion of debt, of payment, and you have in the action called redemption simply a loving God reaching out to his people to free them from a hopeless situation.

This in no way diminishes the absolute need for the saving life and death of Jesus, as we shall see later. This in no way lessens the reality of the terrible weight of sin that the human race carries.

But it does move our ideas of God from legal categories to those of love. Redemption is not an exercise in scale-balancing that God has to go through before he can reach out to us. Redemption is simply and purely an act of God's boundless love.

Because God has liberated people, they now belong to him, not as slaves but as persons called to enter into his life.

WHAT MAN MUST DO: HAVE FAITH

"In the gospel is revealed the justice of God which begins and ends with faith; as Scripture says, 'The just man shall live by faith' " (Rom. 1.17). The "justice of God . . . works through faith in Jesus Christ for all who believe" (Rom. 3.22).

In Paul's view, being human means to yearn for a richness and depth of life which is out of reach. At the same time, being human means being cared for, loved, by God who alone can satisfy the yearning.

What does Paul say that we can do about this, if, indeed, there is anything we care to do or can do?

Paul says "Have faith!"

Faith—another word we have grown up with, but still a word that takes on deeper meaning the more we study it.

The modern religious education movement has worked hard to clarify the meaning of faith. Faith might possibly convey the notion of belief in a body of truths, in a collection of doctrines, in a creed. That is certainly an essential part of its meaning, but there is more.

Faith centers first on a person, Jesus Christ, and then on a body of truths connected with him and his work.

In the biblical sense, "faith" probably comes closer to our word "trust."

Suppose I were learning how to swim. The water is well over my head. The instructor says, "Jump in! Don't worry! I'm standing right here. If you have any problems, I'll throw you a life preserver, or, if necessary, I can jump in and pull you out."

If I do jump in, I trust the instructor with my life. Or, to use biblical language, I have faith in him to keep me from drowning.

Hundreds of times each week, we are asked to put our faith in, to trust, others for all kinds of things in all kinds of ways.

When I come to a cross road where the traffic light is green for me and I keep going at 40 miles per hour, I am putting my faith in those who have the red light not to intrude into my right of way and smash into me.

When parents send their children to school each day, they are putting their faith in a school system, in teachers, to educate their children.

Advertising tries to get us to put our faith in various products.

"Put your faith in this after-shave lotion to make you absolutely irresistible to women."

"Put your faith in this hair coloring to give you the most beautiful and attractive hair."

"Put your faith in this soap to keep you socially agreeable for long periods of time."

"Put your faith in these pills to lessen your headache or sinus problems."

Consciously or unconsciously, we do make what might be called acts of faith in some of these claims, some of these products. Some, with good sense, we refuse to take seriously. And some were never meant to be taken seriously, even by the people who dreamed up the commercials.

The consequences of having faith or not having it can vary. If I cannot have faith that the persons facing the red light will stop, then driving becomes a nerve-wracking ordeal. If parents cannot have faith in the schools to which they send their children, then they carry a burden of worry about the future of those children.

However, men generally survive even if their after-shave lotion does not attract a bevy of beauties. Women somehow come to terms with life even if their new hair color does not make all the people walking down Main Street stop and stare.

However, there is one reality that is of unequaled importance to any person—his or her life.

Everyone has only one life to live. That life is lived according to certain ideas, certain ideals, certain values, even when those are not spelled out fully by the person.

Generally, it is not hard to tell if someone's main direction in life is to make money. Or to be powerful and influential. Or to be popular. Or to have fun. The whole life style, how a person spends time and energy, how he or she treats other people, all of these are the clues to what a person thinks is truly important.

We are surrounded by all kinds of values that beckon to us to accept them as being what life is all about.

"Make money." "Enjoy yourself." "Take care of Number One." "Don't let anyone put anything over on you." "Be one of the beautiful people." "Make everyone recognize you as a success." "Get where people will have to accept you as someone of importance."

These are some of the directions shouted by the world around us.

There are others on another level. "Have a good home and family life." "Make a difference for the better in the world." "Help somebody who needs help."

If we pick the wrong set of values, if we let ourselves be drawn to goals which are poor or false, then—too late—we come to recognize that our life, our only life, has been wasted.

So it becomes necessary to pick that direction in life which is straight and true and leads to what life is truly about.

The Christian challenge is to a special kind of faith. We are called to trust in what God is doing for us through Jesus Christ. Jesus is God making himself known to the world. Jesus is God reaching out to the world to enter into a relationship with men. Jesus is God liberating men from what is cheap and tawdry and less than human. Jesus is God opening up the possibilities for reaching the full measure of humanity.

The Christian challenge is, "Listen to Jesus. Believe him. Follow his way of life. Trust in the gift he brings you."

But there is no way to *prove* that Jesus is the right way. There is no way to *prove* that what he says and does is really what life is all about. There is no way to *prove* that a loving God lives and works in Jesus, or even that there is a loving God. We are called to trust that this is so. This is what is meant by "having faith."

We are called, without being able to convince ourselves or others from indisputable arguments of reason and logic, to profess, "This life I have, this only life, I will live trusting in a God who cares for me and who shows me what he and I are all about through Jesus Christ. This life I have I will live trusting that, through Jesus Christ, God raises me above the only-partially-true or false ways of living that fill the world to the full, rich life that is his."

Faith is not only the acceptance of a truth, but the acceptance of a person who is real to my life now and calls me to listen to him, to love him, to walk with him.

Please read: Romans 4

For Paul, Abraham is the model of faith, the man who shows what faith really means.

In the first of the eucharistic prayers used in the celebration of Mass, the Church refers to Abraham as "our father in faith." Abraham is still set before us as one who can teach us what faith is all about.

The stories about Abraham are told in Genesis 12-24 and a fuller explanation of those stories can be found in another volume of this series. Here we can recall enough of the Abraham story to understand why Paul saw him as the model for a person of faith.

Abraham was called by God to set out from the land in which he lived, had his roots, his family and his possessions. Abraham was to journey to an unknown, distant land. He was to leave what he had of comfort and security at the bidding of a mysterious call whose purpose and meaning were still vague and hidden. He was to trust that God would make of him and his descendants a great nation and give them a land in which to dwell.

As the resettled Abraham and Sarah grew into old age, the great nation that was to be born of them had not even begun to materialize. They had not even one child. But they were still to trust. Eventually that trust was justified when, to an old man and a barren woman, a son, Isaac, was born.

The history of Abraham's faith was still not over. Genesis tells a story of Abraham being tested by God. God summoned him to kill his son, Isaac, as a sacrifice. The son, born after so much difficulty; the son, who carried in himself the only hope of a future people; the son, from whom was to come future generations of descendants for Abraham. For Abraham and Sarah, the birth of Isaac had come in their old age, the result of a last, forlorn hope. If the birth of Isaac was unlikely, the birth of another son would be impossible. And yet Abraham trusted God enough to move to obey what God had demanded. He would blot out the life of this son, who was, after all, God's gift and trust in God for whatever the future might bring. Of course, as the story tells it, he never had to go that far.

Abraham trusted God to bring life from his own body, "which was as good as dead (for he was nearly a hundred years old)" and from "the dead womb of Sarah." Abraham "never questioned or doubted God's promise; rather he was strengthened in faith and gave glory to God, fully persuaded that God could do whatever he had promised."

Because Abraham trusted that God "could bring life from the dead," he is the model for Christians.

The basic act of faith is that true life for all comes from death. God "raised Jesus our Lord from the dead, the Jesus who was handed over to death for our sins and raised up for our justification."

Jesus was raised from the dead by his Father, and in this wonderful act, God made true life possible for everyone.

Paul is at great pains to show that no one can earn this life. No one can reason his way to accepting what God has done.

Abraham did not earn God's promise to him by keeping laws or rules or commandments. God simply called him. Abraham could not prove that conditions would be better for him if he pulled up roots and moved from his ancestral home to a new country. He had simply to accept that the God who had called him would be good to him. Abraham could not foresee what, if anything, would happen if he sacrificed his only son. He simply had to trust that the command and the results of it would be part of God's plan.

The Christian does not earn God's goodness by good works, by keeping rules or commandments. Good works and a good life are the necessary reflection of a relationship with the good God rather than the cause of that relationship. The Christian cannot prove, nor even expect, that, as the world measures things, life will be better as a result of the attempt to listen to and follow God. The Christian cannot prove that Jesus' death had any great significance, that Jesus truly rose from the dead, that Jesus' resurrection opens to all the possibility of true life forever.

Perhaps now the radical nature of faith is clearer.

To believe in the direction God points out for life, above and beyond all those clamoring for our attention, to accept the meaning he put on life, is not simply a matter of study and reason and logic. It is a gift that only God can give. What it involves is being close enough to God through Jesus to be able to say, "I know you enough to trust you, to stake all I have and all I am on you and your word."

SUGGESTIONS FOR REFLECTION

1. One view of "redemption" is a "buying back" of mankind from the slavery of sin through the sacrifice by Jesus on the cross. What idea of God does this imply?

"Redemption" in a biblical sense, is liberating, freeing, saving love. What idea of God does this imply?

How could you help another person who thinks of God as avenging, demanding, and requiring great sacrifice at all costs, and who sees himself as put upon to make up, to atone, to fulfill the demands of such a God?

2. Picture yourself now with one person in your life in whom you have always had implicit faith or trust. Why do you have this feeling or attitude toward this person? Could you prove to someone why you have it? How can this personal relationship help you to have a better understanding of the meaning of faith in God?

Pause a moment to thank God for this person in your life, then make an act of faith or trust in God because of this quality about him that the person has revealed to you. Can you entrust this whole day and night into God's hands?

3. Think over the life of Jesus to reflect on one time when he made clear through words or actions that he had absolute trust in his Father. What were the circumstances demanding such trust? What were the temptations against such trust? What was the outcome when he made the act of trust? What meaning has this event for your own life?

4. Sometimes in the Church we have spoken of doing good in order to earn heaven, to merit reward. There are Catholics who perform holy works because they hope to earn graces. What light do Abraham's faith and trust as a pure gift of God, shed on the idea of "earning graces" or "meriting heavenly reward"? Try to describe what "grace" is; then show how "grace" and "faith" are related to each other.

5. Consider in how many ways God has gifted or "graced" you from your conception down to this very moment of reflection. Take a few moments to respond to him in praise and thanks, realizing that even this capability in you is his gift.

6. At times we use certain theological terms without effort to understand their meanings. Take each of the words: Redemption, Salvation, Faith, and Justice, as this chapter shows them and put them into words that have meaning for your life today.

CHAPTER IV

EVIL IN THE WORLD AND THE GOODNESS OF GOD

From 3.21 to 8.39, Paul's purpose is to describe how God raises mankind from the tragic state described in the first part of the letter. We have already read about God's love which moves through and from Jesus to us.

Now we return again to the problem of evil. We seem to be going back over an already well-beaten path.

This is where an appreciation of Paul's style helps. If we were approaching the problem of evil we might be inclined to use a style that would probably be similar to a straight line. We would state a point, give the arguments to back it up, present explanations and clarifications, then move on to the next point. Each point would be finished before we began a new one. Each issue discussed could be compared to a short, straight line which is connected to other short, straight lines to form a longer line.

Paul's style, which was common in his day, has been likened to a series of concentric circles. A point is made. Then it is repeated in different language, or with additions and explanations. Finally, when it seems the thought has been brought to a conclusion, it is considered still further, with more elaboration and color. This process will go on until Paul, or the author, is satisfied that he has really said all that he wants to say.

This is why, after having already been assured that Jesus frees us from sin and evil, we are once more asked to consider the problem of evil.

THE PROBLEM OF EVIL

Probably one of the most formidable stumbling blocks to belief in a good and loving God is the existence of evil.

How often we hear, think, and perhaps ask questions like, "If God is good, why was this innocent child wasted by sickness?" "If God is good, why did this kind and gentle person have to suffer so much?" "If God is good, why are there wars?" "If God is good, how do you explain those starving children with bloated bellies in so many parts of the world?"

Sometimes the question is very simply but eloquently put as, "Why me?"

I personally have never heard a satisfactory answer to these questions. By that, I mean that I have never heard a response which is so logical, clear and persuasive as well as so emotionally satisfying that I could run out shouting, "Now I understand! Now the mixed-up things in the world make absolute sense."

Our generation is not the first to ask serious questions about evil. Some of the earliest written human documents we possess raise the issue of evil—where it comes from and how we must deal with it. Philosophy and theology over the centuries of human history have grappled with these same questions.

There are at least five questions that focus on evil.

1. Why is there evil in the world?

2. If one believes in God, how is the existence of evil reconciled with the supposed love and goodness of God?

3. Is the evil I do explained by something inside me? Or is there some powerful evil force working outside me which over-

whelms me no matter what my good intentions or how hard I try to do good?

4. Granting that evil is a fact of life, how do I come to terms with it? How do I keep from becoming so frightened and depressed by its power that I am reduced to waiting for oblivion as the only deliverance?

5. Is the good-evil conflict ever settled? Does one of them eventually come out on top? Which one?

People from wisest to simplest have worked out a staggering variety of answers to these questions. They were doing it long before Paul came on the scene. They were doing it in his day. We do it today.

What we are asked to reflect on and to consider accepting as our own is Paul's way of facing up to these questions.

SIN AND DEATH

Please read: Romans 5.12-21

"Through one man sin entered the world and with sin death." "With Adam's sin, God's good creation was spoiled. Humans had now to reckon with death," Paul seems to say.

Here we encounter what theology traditionally calls "original sin."

However, "original sin" is our expression, not Paul's. Much of what might come to mind when we hear the term is not necessarily contained in what Paul writes.

What I am saying is that however legitimate and worthwhile all the later thought and development on the notion of original sin might be, whatever ideas we might have of it, at this moment we are concerned only with what Paul is writing. We will confine ourselves to his ideas, his understanding, his teaching.

30

For example, Paul's attention is not focused on whether there was one set of first parents or several. He is saying nothing about how smart, or beautiful, or talented the first humans were.

THE KEY PERSON: JESUS, NOT ADAM

Even though Paul mentions the story of Adam in Genesis, he does this mainly to contrast him with Jesus Christ. Adam is taken seriously, primarily to provide the background against which to see the bright figure of Jesus.

Adam was "a type of the man to come (Jesus)." This passage compares Adam and his deeds with Jesus Christ and his deeds to stress the superiority of Christ.

While Adam brought death, "much more did the grace of God and the gracious gift of the one man, Jesus Christ, abound for all."

If Adam's sin brought death, "much more shall those who receive the overflowing grace and gift of justice live and reign through the one man, Jesus Christ."

Paul says something about Adam and sin but he says much more about Jesus Christ, about what he accomplished, about the human situation now. However sin and evil came into the world—and Paul with his contemporaries believed literally in the Adam story in Genesis—Paul wishes to talk about the present status of sin and evil, now that Jesus Christ has come on the scene.

THREE IMPORTANT WORDS: SIN, DEATH, SINNER

"Through one man sin entered the world."

Here, sin has a broader meaning than an individual wrong act: a theft, a lie, a murder. It refers to an evil power thriving in the world and actually seeming to be the dominant factor. As

31

we have seen, Sin, with a capital "S," perverts because it turns people from their relationship with God to follow false and shallow goals, ideals, values.

Individual sinful acts are the concrete indications that the evil force is at work in the life of each person. When certain symptoms occur, e.g., fever and nausea, we know that some germ or virus is working inside a person. When you or I hate, or act selfishly, or hurt others, we have experienced the reality of this evil power of sin at work in us.

Death is also to be understood on several levels. Death, simply put, is separation from life. For those who believe, the full measure of life is God, and death is separation from him. This separation can show itself in the many ways that life is choked: in sickness, in personal tragedy, in the lack of justice one experiences. The most obvious sign of being cut off from life is physical death. The lifeless, unfeeling, unmoving corpse is a stark witness that God's life no longer throbs in that vessel of clay. This death points to the ultimate death: lasting, complete separation from God.

— In verse 12, Paul says that this evil power was released into the world by human sinfulness. This evil power pulls all humans to separate themselves from God. Sin, the evil power, has a gruesome companion, Death, which is all the bleak barriers that stand between people and goodness, truth, real life. The most terrifying experience of such a barrier is physical death.

— The evil force, Sin, is so powerful that everyone is inevitably affected by it. Every person commits sinful deeds and thus shows that he or she is under the power of Sin. No one can escape.

A baby born into our world today comes into a situation in which prejudice, hatred, jealousy, selfishness and a jungle of other vices are so luxuriant and tangled, that the child will inevitably be trapped into committing those same sins.

The details of verses 13 and 14 are explained differently by different scholars. However, the main point is clear. Earlier in this letter, Paul painted in broad strokes and divided mankind into two groups, Jews and Gentiles; he affirmed that all humans without exception are corrupted by sin. Now he does the same thing from another point of view. He considers the sinfulness of mankind in the different stages of its history as he understood it.

The first period is from the time of Adam to the time of Moses. Adam, according to the Genesis story, had been given a command, a law, by God. "From the tree of the knowledge of good and evil, you shall not eat." But after Adam, according to the popular view of the Scriptures in Paul's time, there were no more explicit laws given by God to direct mankind.

The second period lasts from the time of Moses to the time of Christ. According to the biblical tradition, Moses was the great lawgiver who presented to the people of Israel God's directions for them in the form of the Ten Commandments and other rules and regulations.

The third period of human history is the time of and since the coming of Jesus Christ.

In the first two periods, from Adam to Moses and from Moses to Christ, it is clear that Sin ruled the world. The proof of this is the fact that all men died. Physical death is the indisputable proof that Sin—separation from God and life—has had its way.

The crucial question is, "What about the third period? What about the time from the coming of Christ on through our own days? Does Sin still rule and cruelly separate men from life?"

From verses 15 through 21, Paul is intent to show his faith that however powerful and frightening Sin might be, what Jesus has done is greater. Life is not hopeless or empty or

destined to futility and despair. Confusion and hatred are
not the victors after all. Jesus Christ is. By his life and death,
he overwhelms and destroys all that stands in the way of true,
lasting and perfect life.

BACK TO OUR QUESTIONS

At the beginning of this chapter, a number of questions were
raised. We can now try to find some answers to these questions
from what Paul says.

Why is there evil in the world?

Because men and women by their own evil acts have put it
there. Because men and women, generation after generation,
add their own pathetic bit of debris to the heap of evil that
they have inherited from the generations before them.

How reconcile evil with a good and loving God?

Evil is man's own work. He must live with the results of what
he has done. Every man sins and his sin carries with it its own
penalty. Sin proves to be most deceitful. It offers promises
that dissolve into dust. Evil is not due to some failure on God's
part. Rather, the wonder is that God still loves and promises
life to his shabby creatures despite their foolish affectations.

Is evil from inside me, or from some power outside me?

There is a combination of both. Every person is born with an
inclination to evil.

But beside this internal inclination to evil, there is also the ac-
cumulated inheritance of evil that is in the world. Ages of hatred, selfishness, ignorance and prejudice have left such an ugly
legacy that every person, burdened with a vulnerability to evil
to begin with, is overwhelmed and sins his own sins.

How do I live with evil?

One person has conquered evil, Jesus Christ, the Son of God. He has also made it possible for every other person to win out over evil also. The next chapter will discuss more fully how this happens. For now it is essential to accept that the way to face evil is to cling desperately to the reality of God's love for each of us and to follow Jesus' trust in his Father despite the apparent pervasiveness of evil. The way to live with evil is to trust that it is not what God intends and offers to us; and to cling to the fact that what God wills for us is good.

Which wins, good or evil?

Good, in the person of Jesus Christ, is the inevitable victor in the struggle. One day sin and death will themselves die. There will be nothing left to block the glorious outburst of God's life and goodness in all of creation.

SUGGESTIONS FOR REFLECTION

1. Have you ever been drawn to ask the questions on pages 29 and 30 because of an event in your life? Share the circumstances with someone if you can. How have you come to terms and lived with your own solutions, i.e., what explanations have you found helpful?

2. When you hear the words "original sin," what definition comes to mind? In what way does it relate to your ideas about sickness, death, heaven, limbo, loss of supernatural gifts, weakened intellect and will, first parents, baptism? How do the ideas you have correspond with Paul's statement in 5.17; "If death began its reign through one man because of his offense, much more shall those who receive the everflowing grace and gift of justice live and reign through one man, Jesus Christ," or in 5. 18, " .. just as a single offense brought condemnation to all men, a single righteous act brought all men acquittal and life."

3. How would you normally describe "death" from your experience? Can you consider personal tragedy or loss, lack of justice, prejudice, or ignorance, change, etc., as forms of death? If we see "separation from life" as a suitable definition of death,

how does "Sin" or separation from God, enter the category of death?

4. "A baby born into our world today comes into a situation in which prejudice, hatred, jealousy, selfishness, and a jungle of other vices are so luxuriant and tangled, that the child will inevitably be trapped into committing those same sins" (p. 32). We have often spoken of original sin as "inherited" and "present in even the smallest baby." How does the new idea present another way of describing the "inheritance" of evil?

5. What are some conditions or signs that prove a thing or person has life? How should these signs be evident in a person to whom Jesus has restored life through his victory over death? Describe how a truly life-filled Christian would show these signs.

6. After reading the weekly newspaper, or hearing a news broadcast, some people feel overwhelmed by the sense of evil in the world. How would Paul's explanation help them to account for it and still live in hope?

CHAPTER V

BEING WITH CHRIST

Perhaps Paul's sentiments in the previous chapter seemed somewhat over-enthusiastic. "Christ has conquered sin and death."

Where?

Evil is still very much alive as far as anyone can see. In fact,
we seem to have gotten much more clever and organized at
hurting one another and our world.

Death is as much a part of human experience as it was in the
years before Christ came. People may live longer than they
used to, but they die just as dead when the time comes.

Even if I take the leap of faith and accept that Jesus Christ rose
from the dead, how does that affect me or anyone else today?
Suppose that Jesus is living now with God the Father. What
difference does that make to me? Does that get me beyond
the evil and death which are as much a part of my experience
and expectation as the rising and the setting of the sun?

CLEVER QUESTIONS

Please read: Romans 6.1-23

Paul begins with an argument he must have heard in various
forms during his preaching and teaching.

The discussion keyed in on what Paul had been teaching
about God as savior. Paul has been emphasizing that

people cannot help themselves where it means the most, in reaching the life to which all our yearning draws us. Paul has stated flatly that people cannot be consistently faithful even to the things they believe to be right.

All are sinners. Salvation is not something that can be earned. It is a gift that only God can give.

So be it! If only God can help, and it is part of his very self to be helping, loving, then the greater a person's sins, the greater will God's goodness be proven to be if he still brings that person to life with himself. In other words, when God gives eternal life to a mass murderer, isn't that much more impressive than when he gives eternal life to a simple, gentle old man whose main faults have been an occasional lie or an unkind word? The more we sin, the more will God demonstrate his love and his mercy when he helps us.

So goes the argument. This is the kind of discussion that develops when the taste for a good argument gets beyond the bounds of common sense.

Paul answers very blunty. "How can we who died to sin go on living with it?" Baptism and faith in Jesus are a kind of dying to a life that takes sin for granted and the beginning of a new life like Jesus' own. To see how, read on.

JESUS' SAVING DEATH

For Paul, Jesus' death is unique. It is not just that Jesus did a noble thing by dying for us. Many heroes have died for causes, country or kin. Jesus' death reached very intimately into the life of every person. His death and resurrection created the possibility for the emergence of a totally new kind of human being.

Jesus' whole life had been one great demonstration of love and obedience to his Father and love for others. That life reached its high point in the death on the cross. There, a whole life of self-offering was summarized in one stark scene.

38

In the Genesis story, Adam insisted on reaching toward God by doing what he wanted to do. Adam refused to trust in God to give him life. He insisted on deciding for himself what life was all about and how he would grasp it.

Jesus obeyed his Father. He listened to him to find how he was to live his life, how he was to serve God's purpose in the world. The gospels relate that Jesus was tempted. Before him dangled the possibility of doing things his own way. "Attract people to yourself by some flashy display of power. Capitalize on the belief of the people that God is going to send them a political and military leader to overthrow their enemies. Swim with the tide that flows in the direction of worldly power and influence." So went the temptation.

But the Father was not calling Jesus to exercise power and influence. The Father is love, mercy, forgiveness, truth. And that was what Jesus was to reveal to the world, not only by his words but by the way he lived and died.

Adam refused to trust that God loved him and would give him life in all its richness. He gave in to the temptation to regard God's truth and direction as an oppressive cover stifling human possibilities.

Jesus was willing to trust God even when such trust seemed misplaced. He was willing to trust that even a disgraceful death on the cross fitted in with God's good plans for him and for the salvation of the world.

The Father raised the trusting, loving, obedient Jesus from death. The Father brought Jesus into eternal life with himself.

THE NEW ADAM

Paul sees Jesus as so unique that he thinks of him in terms of being a "new Adam."

The "old Adam," i.e. the Adam we read about in Genesis, was the founder of a race of people who are like him.

Like Adam, they do not trust God. They do not relate to God as someone who loves them and offers them the kind of life for which everything in them yearns. They do things their own way, set their own meaning on life, make their own decisions about right and wrong. What is all mixed-up here is not that people make their own decisions. This is part of being human. What is horribly twisted is that often these decisions are made without any reference to God.

The "old Adam" acted in a way that alienated him from even his partner, Eve, and from the world in which he lived. Because he made his own decisions without taking into account the God who puts order and peace into the universe, he created conflict between him and his partner and put disorder into the universe. He thought only about himself. This standard for life can lead nowhere except to strife with others who are also thinking only about themselves. This in turn leads to the abuse and rape of the earth in self-serving interests.

Jesus was the "new Adam."

Jesus trusted in God. He accepted God's way of life, even if he might not have understood it totally. With a trust that comes from a close and loving relationship rather than complete understanding, he placed his life in God's hands. He trusted that his Father loved him. If he were faithful to his Father, all that happened to him would work toward the Father's wonderful plan for the universe.

Jesus also loved the people who filled his world. He brought them the good news of the Father's love. He forgave sins and healed sickness as signs of that love.

Those who could not understand him and his message stood against him. The hostility grew as Jesus tried more and more to call all to the Father he was revealing in a new and startling richness.

It soon became clear that the increasing bitterness toward him could move in only one direction, the call for his death.

Still, Jesus had to be true to his Father. He continued his Father's work.

When his fidelity and obedience brought him to the cross, his final words to his persecutors were full of love, selflessness, compassion. "Father, forgive them; they do not know what they are doing" (Luke 23.34).

By his life, death on the cross and resurrection, Jesus became the founder of a new kind of people. The same kind of life that throbbed in him became his gift to those who believe in him and his Father. It is a life of trust, love and obedience to the Father and love for others.

This new life is so real that those in whom it truly flows can no longer dabble with the old life of sin.

How does one step into this new life?

WITH JESUS

The first eleven verses of chapter 6 are filled with expressions that stress a wonderful intimacy with Jesus.

"We were baptized into Christ Jesus." "We were buried with him." "We have been united with him through likeness to his death, so shall we be through a like resurrection." "Our old self was crucified with him." "If we have died with Christ, we believe that we are also to live with him."

How do we get so close to Jesus Christ that we become part of his very life, and he becomes part of us?

BAPTISM

Life is full of signs and symbols.

A flashing red light means danger. A star on a schoolchild's homework means, "Very good." A handshake means, "I greet you as a friend."

Our relationship to God is also full of signs and symbols. In God's own way, these make present his love and care.

One such sign is baptism.

According to Paul, one is brought into the death and rising of Jesus Christ through the rite of baptism.

Here, Paul's interest is not in the obvious symbolism of water washing away sin. Rather, Paul works from the way baptism was conferred in his day. It involved stepping down into a stream or pool, plunging into the water, and then stepping up out of it again.

Going down into the water is like entering a tomb. It signifies death and burial with Jesus. Coming up out of the water is like bursting out of a tomb and signifies the rising to a new life with Jesus. Through baptism, one dies, as Jesus did, to a world filled with sin and evil and rises to a new life with God.

DEATH AND RISING: HOW REAL?

The difficulty with signs and symbols is that the reality does not always keep up with what the sign or symbol is supposed to convey.

While shaking hands may be a conventional sign of friendship, the two persons shaking hands may not really be friends at all, or even willing to explore the possibilities of friendship. The handshake will not make them friends.

The wedding ring on the third finger, left hand, may signify total commitment to another person for life. However, it does not mean, necessarily, that that total commitment is being lived out, nor does the ring by itself make that commitment happen.

However, Paul affirms that the person who has faith and is baptized truly dies to a sin-spoiled life and rises to life with the good God.

WHAT GOES WITH BAPTISM: "JESUS IS LORD"

"For if you confess with your lips that Jesus is Lord, and believe in your heart that God raised him from the dead, you will be saved" (Rom. 10.9).

Such is Paul's description of what must go with the external sign of baptism if one is to enter fully and truly into the new mankind that began with Jesus Christ--faith in Jesus' resurrection; profession that Jesus is Lord.

— What is the significance of professing that "Jesus is Lord?"

The term, "Lord," has a rich background, and all its history contributes to a full understanding.

In Aramaic, the language that Jesus spoke, the word that is translated as "Lord" was "Mar." This was a term of respect reserved for a very important personage, such as a king or a teacher who deserved recognition and honor.

In Hebrew, the language of most of the Old Testament, the word for "Lord" was "Adon" or "Adonai." It carried the general meaning of "Master." But by the time of Jesus and Paul, it had become the characteristic name for God in the Jewish liturgy. God's proper name, Yahweh, was so sacred that it could not be spoken. "Adonai" or "Lord" expressed majesty and respect and so became the substitute word.

In Greek, the word for "Lord" is "Kyrios." (Those over 25 will remember "Kyrie, eleison," "Lord, have mercy"). Generally, to call someone "Kyrios" was a recognition of his authority. By Paul's time, it had become the term of address for a king. This was complicated by the fact that in parts of the world where Paul traveled, kings were recognized, more or less seriously, as having the status of gods. Where this situation prevailed, the idea of loyalty to the king as king and recognition of his divine character went hand in hand.

"Jesus is Lord" became a simple, basic creed which marked Christians off from all others.

The creed professed the absolute authority of Jesus, the claims he made on one's life.

The creed also caused problems.

If Christians insisted that *only* Jesus is Lord, then they would be meeting head-on the civil authorities of the Eastern kingdoms. Christians accepted legitimate civil authority and there was nothing in their belief that would interfere with their being good citizens. However, kings and emperors insisted on being called "Lord." Refusal was treason. Since the term had overtones of divinity, fidelity to their faith would not allow the Christians to recognize divinity in any mere man. Persecution and harrassment were bound to follow.

If Christians insisted on calling Jesus, "Lord," they were certainly going to come into conflict with Jews who were accustomed to use this word in speaking of God. Jews would recognize that Christians were saying that Jesus was on the same level as the God they believed in. How could this be? There is only one God. One of the glories of Israel had been its heroic preservation of belief in one God in the midst of a pagan world.

Yet, "Jesus is Lord" so summed up the faith of Christians that it remained their basic confession.

THE MEANING OF LORDSHIP
When Christians professed, and profess, "Jesus is Lord," there is much at stake.

They express their faith in the reality of Jesus' authority. Jesus shares in the power of God. He rules over time and history with the Father. This is a statement about the present that has tremendous implications for the future.

If it is true that Jesus is Lord, then, despite appearances, despite the experience of here and now, there is no doubt where time and history are heading. The kingdom of peace and love under God that Jesus preached and brought is coming. That is the future for mankind and the universe.

WHERE THE LORDSHIP OF JESUS IS EXPERIENCED

There are at least two intimate experiences of the Lordship of Jesus.

The first is the Eucharist. In the Eucharist, Christians recognize that it is Jesus Christ who has called them together. It is he who makes them all one—men and women, young and old, rich and poor, people of all ethnic and racial backgrounds. The power of Jesus is so great that it overcomes all the barriers that stand in the way of unity and peace. In the Eucharist, Jesus gives all his Spirit, his life, to enable them to live out unity and peace.

The other experience of the Lordship of Jesus takes place within the lives of Christians. To accept Jesus as Lord means to accept him as the one who gives direction to life. This must show in day-to-day decisions and actions. That Jesus is truly Lord for someone is manifest when the signs of the life of his Spirit are present. We can get beyond pious generalities to the specific indications of the presence of Jesus.

"Love, joy, peace, patient endurance, kindness, generosity, faith, mildness, and chastity" (Gal. 5.22-23).

"Love is patient . . . kind . . . not jealous . . . does not put on airs . . . is not snobbish . . . is never rude . . . is not self-seeking . . . is not prone to anger . . . does not brood over injuries . . . . There is no limit to love's forbearance, to its trust, its hope, its power to endure" (1 Cor. 13.4-7).

What Paul has written here is that one comes to baptism believing that Jesus has risen from the dead and willing to profess and live the Lordship of Jesus over the world and history and one's own life.

When this happens, baptism is, in a mysterious yet real way, a death and rising. It is death to a way of life subject to sin and evil. It is rising to a new life filled with the goodness and power of Jesus Christ.

If this is the case, then the superficially clever question posed at the beginning, "Shouldn't we continue to sin, because then, when God saves us, it will be an even greater proof of his love and power?" becomes an obscene joke.

Paul affirms that the new life begins not in some hazy future, but at that moment when a person is gifted by God to commit himself totally to God as he reveals himself through Jesus Christ. From that moment, a new life is born and the beauty and goodness of that life ought to be apparent.

For those who might be wondering how babies can have faith in the resurrection of Jesus Christ and profess that he is Lord, it ought to be mentioned here that Paul was talking about the situation as he knew it. Mature Jews and pagans were accepting the Christian message and adults were being baptized. He does not get directly involved in reflecting on infant baptism.

What he says is true perennially. We die to a life of sin through baptism. We begin a new life because the Spirit of Jesus lives in us. We must affirm that life by our faith in the resurrection of Jesus. We must profess Jesus as Lord and live out his Lordship daily.

SUGGESTIONS FOR REFLECTION

1. We realize that all human beings must die, and as human, so did Jesus. In what way do you see his death as "unique?" How do we today understand the phrase, "obedient unto death" in terms of Jesus' whole life and obedience? In your experience have you ever found peace in obeying God's will, even when you had to "die" to your own will? What was your personal experience when you did something of your own will definitely contrary to God's will?

2. In the context of all that has been said of redemption, salvation, and liberation, why do we speak of Jesus' death as "saving?"

3. If Adam was the "founder" of our human race, in what way is Jesus a "new Adam?"

4. When a human being is born he takes on the condition of the whole race, the inevitability of death. How does baptism (seen by Paul as immersion) demonstrate in ritual and ceremony our belief that even the inevitability of death is not final?

5. It is difficult for many people to think of God as "good," especially when they reflect on Jesus' death. What argument does Paul use to prove that God *is* good and wants only the good for all his creatures?

6. If "Jesus is Lord" is the creed that professes the "absolute authority of Jesus", over each of our lives, recall a time in your life in which he made such a claim over you that you literally acknowledged him as Lord of your life. Has another person or thing ever made lordship demands on your life? What did you do about it? How was your response like or unlike that of the early Christians?

7. Why is it an appropriate prayer to say, "Jesus is Lord" before and after reading the daily newspaper, listening to the news, looking at your watch, beginning and ending work, play,

and prayer? What effect could such a thought have on the way you live your leisure time?

8. When you look around the church before Mass next Sunday, let your eyes focus on each person there. Then connect them with the prayer, "Jesus is Lord" and what is about to happen.

9. Baptism signifies dying and rising in the physical order as well as in every day's life. Name several "dying" examples in your life; mention some "rising" occasions in your life. What form did your last "dying-rising" take?

CHAPTER VI

REASON TO HOPE

Those who like things tied up very neatly and tidily might begin to feel a little uneasy here.

Presuming a basic commitment to God in and through Jesus, when do we finally grow up? When do we stand on our own two feet? When do we, so to speak, cut loose from God's apron strings and do the right things on our own?

The ideal human situation develops when parents give life to a child, care for, educate, protect it, but gradually help it to become a mature human making its own decisions and facing life as a mature adult. There would be something very wrong with a thirty-five year old man or woman running home to mother or father every time there was need to make an important decision.

Would not the ideal situation be that God shows us the way, helps us along, and then says to us, "Now the rest is up to you"?

After all, God has given us a way of life in the teaching of Jesus. He has given us the example of Jesus. What we needed were some pointers, some directions. Now we can just go and do.

Paul has touched on this question previously, but it still bothers him. According to his style, which does not require that every issue or point be dealt with all in one place, Paul comes back to the question of whether people ever really come of age to the extent of standing independently of God.

WHAT THE LAW MEANS

Please read: Romans 7.1-25

Paul seems to be waging a running battle with "the Law," not only in this letter, but also elsewhere, notably in the letter to the Galatians.

What is "the Law," and why is Paul so down on it?

The Law suggests a number of realities which overlap.

The Law is the whole vast body of rules and regulations found in the Hebrew Scriptures, by which a devout Jew would direct his life. The Law also included the interpretations of the rules and regulations given by learned and devout rabbis.

By keeping these laws, and following the interpretations of them, one worked toward salvation.

But Paul sees a meaning in Law which goes beyond the Old Testament, but of which the Old Testament is a supreme illustration.

Law is direction for living, for conduct. Law says, "Do this" and "Don't do that." Any law can be good, and God's Law ought to be very good.

The problem is that any law, even God's, is a guide which points the way but does not provide any help to move in that direction.

Suppose I buy a bicycle that has to be assembled. The directions for putting it together are included in the box.

But suppose that I am hopelessly inept at any kind of mechanical work. I pore over the instructions. I struggle with wrench and screw-driver, with wheels, handlebars, pedals. Still I produce nothing more than a clutter of parts, and finally give up in despair.

The instructions were a "Law." They were a set of directions which told me what to do. As such they were good. But in no way did they make up for my own lack of mechanical ability. Hence, I produced not a bicycle but a junk pile.

FREEDOM FROM LAW

Paul says that "we have died to the law," "we have been released from the law."

Freedom from the law became necessary because, paradoxically, even God's law became an occasion of sin.

Paul sums up God's law as "You shall not covet." "Covet" catches the essence of temptation. One is attracted to the illusion of being totally free and independent. This is what one grasps at, covets. To decide all by oneself what one will be, what one will do, seems like such a pleasant prospect. Not to be tied down by parents, or spouse, or country, or domineering God.

Of course, such an attitude totally ignores the kind of God we believe in—a God who is good and loving. It also ignores the kind of beings we are—made so that only God satisfies what we most deeply yearn for. Snatching at anything less than him brings only disappointment.

Yet, we are still tempted to "covet." And "You shall not covet" expresses what God expects; trust, love obedience.

A believer will not quarrel with the goodness of this law. But the fatal flaw in law is still present. Being told not to covet does not give the help not to covet. In fact, once a person knows what a proper relationship to God is all about and fails to live up to it, his sin is greater because he acts not out of ignorance but out of the knowledge that what he is doing is wrong.

THE LAW AND "I"

Verses 15 through 24 are a classic passage.

In them, the "I" who speaks sums up the experience of all human beings.

"I cannot even understand my own actions. I do not do what I want to do but what I hate . . . the desire to do right is there but not the power. What happens is that I do, not the good I will to do, but the evil I do not intend."

The "I" is not Paul specifically but includes all people in all periods of history. That the discription is an accurate one is verified by our own experiences. I dare say most of us would agree, "That's exactly the way it was with me. Everything in me cried out that I should not do such and such, that it was wrong. Yet I just went ahead and did it. And now all I feel is shame and guilt. And I know it will happen that way again."

The whole frustrating experience is summed up exactly. "What a wretched man I am! Who can free me from this body under the power of death?"

By now we have read enough of St. Paul to know that he has not contemplated once again human sinfulness and entrapment by evil simply because he is miserable and "Misery loves company."

Paul stresses how bad things are so that we will appreciate how good things are. He has appealed to experience to make us realize how much evil there is around, and within, us. He has made us face the fact that this is a poisonous combination, devastatingly destructive. He has brutally tried to make us accept the fact that, by ourselves, we are helpless.

Now he would give us something else—*Hope.*

He would help us to open our hearts to the God who loves us and so face the present and the future not with despair but with confidence and a sense of purpose.

FLESH

Please read: Romans 8.1-12

"Flesh" can convey different meanings. For someone on a diet, flesh is the extra poundage to be gotten rid of. For someone who is the product of a certain kind of upbringing, "sins of the flesh" would probably suggest failures in the area of sexual morality.

For Paul, flesh (the Greek word is *sarx*) means something rather different. It refers not to body as opposed to soul, or sexuality. Flesh means the whole self as considered from a specific point of view.

Isaiah 40.6-8 reads:
"All mankind (literally: "flesh") is grass,
and all their glory like the flower of the field.
The grass withers, the flower wilts,
when the breath of the LORD blows upon it.
[So then, the people is the grass.]
Though the grass withers and the flower wilts,
the word of our God stands forever."

Here, "flesh" is used to describe humanity as frail, weak, here-today-gone-tomorrow in contrast to the ever-living God, whose word is eternal.

Paul uses the word with a similar meaning. To say, "Mankind is flesh" does not by itself say that the human race is evil. It is a statement of the fact that no human can stand alone, that he is a creature, that, next to God, he is small and feeble.

No person, left alone, can soar beyond frailty and limitation.

But, in the drama as Paul narrates it, "fleshly" humanity has a mortal enemy in Sin. Sin, as we saw before, is an evil force working both in every person as individual and in the human race all together, to frustrate God's good purpose for his creation.

53

People as "flesh" are absolutely no match for the power of sin.

—"Those who live according to the flesh are intent on the things of the flesh" portrays the earth-bound person, head bowed, facing the ground, the heavy burden of sin on his back, unable to stand up straight, unable to look at and reach for the wonders that God has intended.

SPIRIT

Again, as with flesh, this word, "spirit," does not mean some part of a person, the soul. Rather, "spirit" (the Greek word is *pneuma*) signifies the whole person seen from another point of view.

Spirit is a person to the extent that that person is open to receive from God the life of God himself. Spirit is a person able to realize all that God intends because God has lifted him, or her, out of the grip of Sin.

"BY THE SPIRIT, YOU WILL LIVE"

This is Paul's first hope-filled promise.

Law means obligations and directions for life which point out the right way, but which give no power to move along that way. The people on whom this Law is laid, while often able to recognize the rightness of God's Law, are in a terrible combat with a power within and around them. They are no match for this power. Hence, the results of the unequal struggle are inevitable.

However, there is a new "law," the "law of the spirit." This is different from any other kind of law because it carries the help to live up to it. This new law is the way of Jesus Christ, the way of love. The help is the life of Jesus himself. As difficult as it is to explain and understand, Jesus imparts something of his own life to us so that we can live the way he did.

This life of Jesus, flourishing within those who give themselves to him, will ultimately overcome everything that oppresses mankind. Because this shared life is God's life and God lives forever, even death will be eliminated. The person who lives in the spirit will live forever.

SONS OF GOD

Please read: Romans 8.14-17

Here we have Paul's second promise.

"All who are led by the Spirit of God are sons of God. You did not receive a spirit of slavery leading you back into fear, but a spirit of adoption through which we cry out, 'Abba!' (that is, 'Father')."

God is referred to a number of times in the Old Testament as "Father." Calling God "Father" stresses especially his great love for his people, his mercy and forgiveness even in the face of the sinfulness and lack of gratitude of his people.

The rabbis of Jesus' time also called God "Father" on occasion. They would allow the person who obeys God's Law to address him with this word. But God's fatherhood would include also his love which has no limits and goes far beyond any human faults.

However, and this is an extremely important point, the word for Father used by the Old Testament and by the rabbis at the time of Jesus is a formal one. The tone might best be conveyed in our culture if we imagined a small child addressing its father as "Father," rather than as "Dad" or "Daddy."

Furthermore, there is no indication that anyone up to the time of Jesus referred to God as "my Father." The general idea is that God is "our Father," i.e., the Father of the people as a group.

Jesus speaks to God in an original and unique way. He speaks of God as "*my* Father," and to address God he uses not the formal word for Father but the word which appears in this text, "Abba."

"Abba" is a word of familiarity and endearment. It is calling one's father "Dad," rather than the more dignified, and perhaps less intimate "Father."

When we find Jesus using this term for his Father, he is addressing God in terms of great intimacy, secure in the intensity of the relationship between him and the Father. He accepts with simplicity that he is close to God in a way that no one else is. Because Jesus stands so close to God, he makes him known to others in a way that cannot be matched.

Although only Jesus can by right use this title of intimacy to speak of and to God, he invited those who follow him to use the same word. He opened up for all people the possibility of intimate, secure, familiar relationship with God.

Because we are "sons of God" in this sense of the term, we also become "heirs of God, heirs with Christ." The destiny waiting for us is a never-ending share in the perfect life of the Father.

THE LIBERATION OF THE WORLD

Please read: Romans 8.19-22

Here we meet the third of Paul's promises.

The biblical tradition insists that there is a close connection between what happens to people and what happens to the rest of the universe. Because man and woman sin, God's plans for the rest of creation are somehow thrown into confusion. In the story in Genesis, because of the sin of Adam and Eve, the earth began to bring forth thorns and thistles instead of the good fruit it was meant to produce. How the connection works is mysterious, but it is nonetheless there.

The process also moves in the other direction. As human beings become more filled with God's spirit, as they become more God's sons, as they move toward being what God intended them to be, so they affect the rest of creation for the better. Eventually the whole created universe will reach that situation of peace and harmony that God intended. How this will happen, we cannot say. Nor can we describe what a transformed universe might be like or what living in an ideal world might be. What we can say is that the final destiny of creation is closely linked to the destiny of mankind.

This has important consequences for our times. Perhaps as no generation before us, we are aware of the effect that we are having on the world around us. We have been warned that pollution, litter, abuse of the resources of the earth, waste of energy, could make this planet unlivable in the not-too-distant future.

Paul speaks to our situation.

Whatever programs governments and environmentalists and in-dividuals might inaugurate, we are still faced with the need to become what God intended us to be. Unless we recognize our own relationship to God and to one another, unless we recog-nize that our world has been given to us for the common good of all and not for the luxury of a few, unless we recognize our responsibility for one another and for all creation, we will in-evitably lapse into selfish and spoiling abuse of our world.

Unless we accept the relationship of love and concern that God intends to exist among people, including those in future genera-tions, we will see nothing wrong in stripping the earth for our own selfish needs. We will see nothing wrong in littering roads and parks as long as we have our own neat, fenced-in quarter acre, or our own spotless apartment. Unless we believe and live the belief that we are responsible for one another, we will not be troubled by the terrible inequality which allows the wealthy of the world to watch on color television the starvation of the poor.

Paul holds out a sign of hope to a world that is just beginning to realize the terrible consequences that may come from the wasteful and irresponsible use of technology and resources. Everything can be, and will be, peaceful, harmonious, in order.

But the only way that this will happen is when humans open themselves to the life of God in the Spirit.

EVERYTHING HELPS

Please read: Romans 8.28-30

"God makes all things work together for the good of those who have been called."

In modern parlance, this is truly a mind-blowing idea. Everything, good or bad, big or small, in some way fits together in bringing a person to life with God. The thought is too much for us. Caught up in the joy of a moment, struggling with the pain of a moment, we cannot see with the vision of God. His vision is not limited to moments but includes all of time and history in one sweep.

The joy of an experience of love, of friendship, of kindness, of beauty, helps us to appreciate these qualities in God.

The pain of sickness, of family troubles, of death, reminds us not to put our trust in the here and now but to be open to the fulness which only God can bring. The moments of pain are challenges and opportunities for us to live out our trust in God, our call to service, our belief in the future he promises.

By the way, we should not get side-tracked by the language in this passage—God "predestined." The term does not have the same meaning that later theological controversies will give it. Paul is simply stating that all those who accept and grow in the life of God's Son are called to that life by him. Paul does not discuss God's excluding anyone from such a call.

GOD'S LOVE

Please read: Romans 8.31-39

This magnificent passage sums up what Christian hope is all about. God reveals his love by sending his own Son to live on earth and to die for people. In the face of this overwhelming testimony to God's love, it should be clear that, on God's part, there is nothing to stand between us and him.

Obstacles to a loving union with God must therefore come from us and from the world in which we live. But not even these can stand as barriers to Christ's love which pursues us incessantly.

No human weakness, like trial, or hunger, or danger can interfere with Christ's love. No superhuman powers (Paul is using the popular language of his day, "angels," "principalities," "height," "depth") can ever block the love God has for us.

If this is the truth, then we indeed have reason for rejoicing because of what God's love has made us and for hoping because of what God's love will make us.

SUGGESTIONS FOR REFLECTION

1. If law is right direction for living and for conduct, and if the Ten Commandments are meant to be just that, then why is it difficult for many persons to find fulfilment and life in observing this Law alone?

2. Although the Law was given by God and as such was good, Paul saw it as an "occasion of sin." Explain how it is possible even today for the Law of God to be an occasion of sin.

3. How is the manner of observance of the Law indicative of a person's relationship with an idea of God?

4. Paul's idea of "flesh" in contrast to "spirit" has been frequently misunderstood to mean "body" in contrast to "soul." Explain how we now realize Paul's meaning in these two terms, with its implications for true life.

5. Have you ever found yourself doing an action of love almost in spite of yourself, as though impelled by the life of Jesus, and not your own? Why doesn't this happen all the time? How

can you let it happen more often?

6. In contrast to "the Law" of the Old Covenant, why do we consider the "Law of the Spirit" of the New Covenant to be hope-filled?

7. What effect should the life of Jesus have on those who live according to the Spirit?

8. How does Jesus' calling God "Father" differ from the way the word was used by the Pharisees? Explain how we are affected by the same relationship. What is the role of the Spirit in enabling this relationship? Is the love of God our Father for us diminished by our human faults? How does our being "sons of God" entitle us also to be "heirs of God"? When we speak of "inheriting the kingdom" what really do we mean? Take some time to reflect on the meaning of this great promise for your life today.

9. Have you ever had the experience of feeling that you are related to the natural world of creation—plants, animals, rocks, soil? Have you ever had the experience of feeling that you are related to other human beings than your own family? If so, try to describe the circumstances. Do thse personal experiences help you to understand better how our evil or good deeds can have an effect beyond ourselves in the universe? How can we give our children an early taste of this sense of relationship to all creation?

10. If mankind were to realize its relationship to the generations of the past and future, how would it regard its responsibility for use of the earth's resources? What does Paul mean when he describes all creation as "groaning" to be freed? Have you ever made do with less or refused to use something of the earth's resources to make it possible for others to have more? Explain how. During the energy crisis many persons deliberately conserved because of a new consciousness. How can we raise people's consciousness of responsibility for others and of the need for a new life in the Spirit?

11. What connection have human life in the Spirit, and human sonship in God with bettering the condition of all creation? Why do you think so many programs for conservation of resources and energy have failed in the past?

12. Even in our lifetime we sometimes see how God is bringing us to life with him through experiences of pain or suffering. If you have had such an experience, reflect on it with gratitude. It might help someone else to share it.

13. "The joy of an experience of love, of friendship, of kindness, of beauty, helps us to appreciate these qualities in God." Reflect upon your experience of one of these to see what it reveals to you of what God is like.

14. Paul gives us here a God's-eye view of time by warning us against putting our trust in the present, and in recommending belief in the future God promises. What is the meaning of this for your life today?

15. Sometimes in the midst of trials people feel that God is far from them or has abandoned them. After reading how nothing can separate us from the love of God manifested in Christ Jesus, how would you console such persons?

CHAPTER VII

PAUL AND THE JEWS

Please read: Romans 9.1-11.36

Paul must now come to terms with what is for him a burning issue. He has just described the sinful status of the human race and God's response to that through the death and resurrection of Jesus. He has explained how men and women become sharers in God's loving plan to rescue them from sin and bring them to perfect life.

But Paul faces a fact of history. His own people, the Jews, were largely unable to accept the message of and about Jesus. While it is true that the first followers of Jesus were Jews and that a good number of Jews came into the early Church, the reality was that the great majority of Jews rejected Jesus as the Christians understood him and his role. In fact, Paul met with hostility and even persecution from some Jews to whom he preached during his travels.

THE PROBLEMS CAUSED BY THIS FAILURE

That so few Jews had been able to accept Jesus as the Lord, as the fulfillment of God's promises of good, caused Paul great personal pain. In his letters, Paul boasted of being a Jew. "I myself am an Israelite, descended from Abraham, of the tribe of Benjamin" (11.1). He had grown up a pious Jew and no doubt had fond memories of the many Jews who had impressed him with their goodness and had filled his early life with their piety and traditions. Now Paul had come to know Jesus as the culmination of all that the Jews were waiting for. Why was it that so many of his Jewish friends, so many of those whom he respected and admired, could not accept Jesus as he had?

Paul puts his feelings this way. "There is great grief and constant pain in my heart. Indeed, I could even wish to be separated from Christ for the sake of my brothers, my kinsmen the Israelites" (9.2-3).

Does the fact that most Jews have not accepted Jesus mean that Israel has been rejected by God? This cannot be true! God had called these people—"Theirs were the adoption, the glory, the covenants, the law-giving, the worship and the promises; theirs were the patriarchs, and from them came the Messiah."

They had been the channel of his saving work. In the face of pagan surroundings, persecution and disaster, despite lapses into infidelity, they had kept alive belief in the one true God.

How would God be faithful to his word if these people were now to be cut off from the peace and salvation to which their history was intended to lead? How could God really be loving if those for whom, through spokesmen like Moses and the prophets, he had professed his love over the centuries, were now no longer to feel that love?

THE BASIC PRINCIPLES

Paul speaks to these questions which are real and painful for him.

There were no neat and totally satisfactory answers but Paul keeps returning to two basic principles.

The first principle is that *he is not discussing salvation and damnation.* Paul is not talking about Jews going to heaven or hell. He is not talking about what might or might not happen to individual Jews. He is talking about a people and the role that they play in the working out of God's plan of salvation as he saw it. Paul leaves the question of who comes to God where it belongs—in the mysterious realm of the overpowering love and mercy of God. What he tries to deal with is a sketch of God's saving activity insofar as the events of human history show it working out.

The second principle is that we are dealing with the *mystery of God's freedom.* How and through whom God chooses to work is something which is ultimately beyond our comprehension. This is not a tricky sidestep away from an embarrassing issue. We must honestly face the difference between our own small, limited understanding of what is happening and God's unlimited all-seeing vision.

GOD'S FREEDOM AT WORK   (Romans 9.6-13)

Paul reaches for two examples from the Hebrew Scriptures to illustrate God's freedom.

Abraham was the recipient of promises made by God that he would be the father of a new people and that he would be a source of blessing to all humankind. He had two sons who could take his place. His first son was Ishmael, born of his wife's servant girl. The second son, Isaac, was by his aged wife, Sarah. Of the two, God chose Isaac to be the one to carry on his promises. God freely chose Isaac over Ishmael for his own purposes.

Paul is sensitive to the weakness of this example.

Of course Isaac, the son of Abraham's legitimate wife, would be regarded as the proper heir over Ishmael, the son of a concubine, even if Ishamel were older.

Paul moves to another example.

Esau and Jacob were the twin sons of Isaac and his wife, Rebecca. Esau was the first to be born. They were both sons of the same rank, and by all the rules of inheritance, Esau should have been the legitimate heir, the carrier of the promises God had made. But even before they were born, before either had done anything either good or bad, Genesis says that God indicated that Jacob and not Esau would be the one to preserve the promise.

One brief comment on Paul's quotation from the prophet, Malachi—"I have loved Jacob and hated Esau."

This needs interpretation because it sounds very harsh. After all, God hating somebody! For proper understanding, it helps to know that the Hebrew language finds it very difficult to express comparatives. Its peculiarities as a language make it difficult to say something like, "I have loved Jacob more and loved Esau less." Yet this is more the meaning of this statement. And even this could do with further clarification.

Paul actually interprets what the statement means in verse 12, quoting from Genesis 25.13, "The older shall serve the younger." In his wisdom, God has seen fit to use Jacob rather than his brother Esau to carry out his intentions. This is not to condemn Esau, but simply to state that God's plan is his and not ours.

AN OBJECTION: GOD IS BEING ARBITRARY

(Romans 9.14-18)

"Well, then, God is being unjust! Nothing we do counts for anything. We are helpless in his hands."

Such is the reaction that we might have to a God presented in these terms. And such is the reaction that Paul had probably heard and was ready for.

He recalls another key incident from the history of Israel.

In the stories in Exodus about the escape from Egypt, two men, Moses and Pharaoh, play key roles.

Moses is God's spokesman, the leader who tells the people and the Pharaoh what is happening and why. Through Moses, God most obviously reveals what he is doing for his people who are about to break out from their slavery.

The hard-hearted Pharaoh stands in the way of the demands

conveyed by Moses for freedom for God's people. It takes the plagues to force Pharaoh to let the people go. After they have fled, he regrets what he has done and pursues with an army to bring them back.

Strangely enough, even the stubbornness of Pharaoh reveals the power of God. The Exodus story would be far less impressive if Moses had gone to Pharaoh and said, "Release the Hebrew slaves," and Pharaoh had responded, "Fine! You may leave whenever you are ready." The fact that Pharaoh resisted and raised all kinds of obstacles to the departure of the Hebrews brought into even clearer relief the power of God. God's power to free his people surpassed even the might of the king of Egypt who was determined not to free them. Even the king of Egypt and his nation were forced to recognize that something greater than they was at work. They had tried to stand in the way of that something greater, and found that it overwhelmed them.

The obstinacy of Pharaoh and his determination not to give in to Moses ultimately became an illustration of the power of God and his intention to save his people.

Thus, these two men both served God's purposes—Moses, by cooperating with God's plans; Pharaoh, by trying to block those plans. And there is, even here, still no question of eternal salvation or damnation.

AN EVEN LOUDER OBJECTION (Romans 9.19-24)

"If God really acts this way, then nobody is personally responsible for anything. God just overwhelms each person and makes that person do what he wants, either good or bad."

Here Paul returns to the basic principle of God's freedom. We cannot understand his ways. Through all of this letter, Paul has been asserting that God's conduct is purposeful and not arbitrary, or bizarre, or fickle. But we simply cannot hope to understand all about how his purposes work out.

A potter can take a lump of clay, cut it in two, use one half for a magnificent decorative vase and the other half for a water cup. God can also use people to fulfill his ultimate purpose in different ways. Even the fact that most of the Jews did not accept Jesus in some way fits into God's plan.

THE FAILURE OF ISRAEL   (Romans 10.1-21)

The glory of his Jewish contemporaries, as Paul saw it, was that they truly cared for the one true God. Their failure lay in their unwillingness to let this God break through the limits they had set for him. They tried to remain faithful to his laws and they tried to hope in the future he had promised them. But they could not accept that this promised future was upon them in the presence of Jesus.

The message of Jesus had been preached to them and they had been unable to accept it. Non-Jews had been more receptive.

THE PLACE OF ISRAEL IN GOD'S PLAN:
THE "REMNANT"   (Romans 11.1-10)

Throughout Israel's history, the prophets had offered both warning and hope.

The warning was directed at the failures of the people to be faithful to God. At times, many turned away from the one true God to follow false gods. Many neglected their responsibilities to one another. Many made of religion a flimsy tissue of ceremonial observances without substance. Because of this, their land, their temple, their king, would be lost. So said Amos and Hosea, Isaiah and Jeremiah.

But in the words of the prophets, there were also rays of hope. One such ray of hope was the theme of the remnant.

A remnant is, obviously, that which is left over from something. The prophets used the term to refer to a portion of the people. Whenever there was a multitude unfaithful to God, bringing God's judgment on themselves and causing their own destruction, there was also another group open to hear God, to follow where he might lead. This group was the sign of God's continu-ing love.

The remnant was that portion of the people whom God's goodness and grace kept faithful to him and whom he preserved even in the midst of the worst disasters that befell Israel.

Paul understands himself and those others from among the Jews who have accepted Jesus as Lord as the remnant. Most Jews could not accept that God's ultimate salvation would be in and through Jesus. A relatively small body of Jewish Christians followed God's call down this new path. These constituted the remnant.

THE PLACE OF ISRAEL: PROD TO THE
GENTILE MISSION   (Romans 11.11-32)

Seeing with a vision that could only be inspired by a serene faith, Paul reflects that the general rejection of Jesus by the Jews of his day has actually had an unexpected positive effect.

Much of the non-Jewish world looked on the Jews with suspicion and even contempt. If the Christian message had been generally accepted by the Jews, Christianity would have kept a very definite Jewish character. Christian missionaries would have been considered as bringing another kind of Judaism. The prejudiced and bigoted of the ancient world would have been much less likely to listen.

Furthermore, the very fact of rejection and persecution forced the first Christians to move out into the non-Jewish world. If they had been accepted generally by the Jews, there was the distinct possibility that the Christians would have been content to stay where they were, working among those of Jewish background. The universal movement to the rest of the world might have been delayed. The Acts of the Apostles presents the spread of the Church in terms whereby Jesus, about to ascend into heaven, says, "You are to be my witnesses in Jerusalem,

through Judea and Samaria, yes, even to the ends of the earth"
(Acts 1.8). It is important to recognize that, as Acts relates
the spread of the word, persecution is the cause of this three-
step movement. Persecution of the Christians in Jerusalem
forces them to scatter through Judea and Samaria (8.1-3).
When Paul appears in Rome, the prophecy is fulfilled. Rome,
the capital of the political world, is "the ends of the earth."
Paul has gotten to Rome because of Jewish objections to his
preaching which resulted in his imprisonment and his appeal
to be judged by the Roman authorities.

As painful as the failure of the Christian mission to the Jews
might have been to Paul, he could still see with the eyes of
faith. Even this failure mysteriously worked into God's plan.
It resulted in a more widespread, more active mission to the
non-Jews.

THE PLACE OF ISRAEL: THE FUTURE (Romans 11.11-12)

Paul cannot see the details of the future. However, he is certain
that God's plans for the Jews include a turning to him in and
through Jesus. How and when this will happen, Paul cannot
say. But he is sure that this conversion will occur. When it
does, it will mark the final stage of God's call to them.

Paul then recalls once more the glorious privileges of the ancient
Israelites. They were called to play a unique role in God's saving work. That call has not ceased. The gift of salvation still
blossoms from their roots. However, non-Jews have been
grafted into that fine old tree to replace those who could not
grow in the direction that God intended. This is not an occasion
for non-Jewish Christians to boast or belittle the Jews. It is a
challenge to them to reflect seriously on their own openness to
the movement of God.

A HYMN TO THE MYSTERIOUS WORKINGS
OF GOD   (Romans 11.33-36)

This has been a difficult section. It has been personally difficult for Paul to try to fit together the whole past history of the Jews with their rejection of Jesus.

It has been emotionally difficult for Paul to find himself so estranged from his own people.

This section is also very difficult for us. The issue of Jewish-Christians relations in our own day makes this topic a very delicate one. The attempts to understand God's workings can no doubt leave us unsatisfied and puzzled. Paul's theological explanations have been very complex, filled with references to the Old Testament. We have tried to trace only the general lines of his treatment. We have deliberately left aside modern ecumenical questions in favor of an exposition of Paul's thought.

With Paul, we might well conclude with a statement of our wonder at God and his greatness and of our own inability to grasp that wonder and greatness. We can recognize "how inscrutable his judgments, how unsearchable his ways."

At the same time, we ought to recognize that this mystery about God is most truly a mystery of his "riches and wisdom and knowledge." What is mysterious about God is the greatness of his love and his power, both directed to our benefit.

And from the hymn, we might move to a consideration of our own lives. How well have we been able to fit failure, trouble and pain, along with success and joy, into a life which is directed to receiving God's salvation for ourselves and to being an instrument of that salvation to others? Does our vision of God's work allow even for failure, real or apparent, in and around the Church?

SUGGESTIONS FOR REFLECTION

1. Paul suffered much heartbreak in the rejection of Jesus by his own people, the Jews, whom he loved and who were his traditional family as he grew up. In today's family life parents sometimes experience a rejection of their religious beliefs by a

70

loved member of the family, a child, or by a respected teacher or friend. How could this portion of the epistle to the Romans throw light on understanding and bearing this human experience? If God is capable of making all things work together unto good, how might parents and other religious persons live in patience with this problem?

2. At times we wonder why people who have had the same basic religious upbringing and training as we cannot as adults accept Jesus and the Church. How does Paul's Chapter 9 throw light on this question?

3. Paul, to whom Christ was literally everything, was in such agony over the rejection by his own people, that he would even have become separated from him if he thought it could bring about a reconciliation. Have you ever felt this way, or experienced a similar sense of helplessness in reconciling a relationship? Share this experience with someone, telling also its outcome.

4. God has made the covenant with and given his promises to his chosen people. Even though many did not believe in his Son, how did God show himself to be faithful to his word to the Israelites? Does God forget his promise when an individual person is no longer faithful?

5. What are the two basic principles Paul assumes in his discussion in Chapter 9 of the epistle to the Romans?

6. At times we tend to think of the most eligible person according to our standards as the one God will choose for his work. How do the illustrations about Ishmael and Isaac, and Esau and Jacob disprove this idea? How could you explain that in this God is not unjust?

7. Should the statement "I have loved Jacob and hated Esau" really be taken literally as we would mean it today? Does God ever hate anyone?

8. As the story of Moses and the Pharaoh proves, God's purposes will be served either by man's cooperation with his plans, or by man's resistance to his plans. Recall other instances in the Bible when men tried to block God's will, but were unsuccessful. What was the outcome? Have you seen this same phenomenon at work in your own life? What does it tell us of man's freedom and of God's freedom?

9. The expectations for a Messiah on the part of Paul's Jewish contemporaries were different from the kind of Redeemer God sent. Much pain is present in the post-Vatican Council II period of the Church because peoples' expectations are different from the way the Spirit has acted. In your life have your expectations of how God should or would act ever been different from the way he did act? How can you personally become less tied to your own expectations and more open to his action?

10. Many Catholics today are upset by the seeming fall-out of membership in the Church and fall-off of attendance at services. How might the Jewish experience of "remnant people" prove hopeful for them?

11. Sometimes God works to achieve a greater success through our failures of the moment, as he did through the Jewish rejection of the early Christian mission. Describe how this has been true in your own faith life and experience.

12. Commit the hymn of 11.33-36 to memory and use it as a prayer to be pondered by you in terms of your own life, both in the family and in the parish.

CHAPTER VIII

THE LAST WORDS

Please read: Romans 12.1-15.27

Paul, following his usual style, now offers some reflections about the practicalities of Christian life. The first eleven chapters have been an extensive theological survey. Paul now reaches into everyday life to describe the kind of persons he has depicted in his letter, persons who have been caught by Sin, but have now been released from that trap and live in Jesus Christ.

The themes of the Church as the Body of Christ (12.3-8) and the demands of Christian love (12.9-21) have already been treated in more detail in the booklet on First Corinthians.

What is interesting to note here is how much of chapters 12-13 is similar to the material gathered in the "Sermon on the Mount" (Matthew 5-7). Romans 12.14-21 should be read together with Matthew 5.38-48. Matthew 5.21 ff. takes a number of commandments and explains how they must be observed in a new way by Christians. Paul also mentions commandments: "You shall not commit adultery; you shall not murder; you shall not steal; you shall not covet." He affirms how all of these are summed up in one commandment, "You shall love your neighbor as yourself."

In a similar vein, Jesus is depicted as saying, in Matthew 5.17, that he has come not to abolish the Law and the prophets "but to fulfill them." Paul writes here that "love is the fulfillment of the law."

THE CHRISTIAN AND THE STATE   (Romans 13.1-7)

This is the only place in the letters where there is any detailed instruction on the relationship of the Christian to the state.

Paul would naturally think of saying something about the state when he wrote to Rome. After all, Rome was *the* state. The Roman Empire was the all-pervasive reality of his day. Its power and influence reached into all corners of the world. Paul and the people he had met in his travels knew Rome, paid its taxes, were subject to its laws.

It is also quite possible that the Christians, as members of what would have been considered a strange and exotic religion, might have been suspected of disloyalty to Rome. As we have seen, the basic Christian profession of faith, "Jesus is Lord," made it impossible for them to recognize kings and emperors as "Lord." Was this refusal to render the title, "Lord," to an earthly king a sign that they would not obey that king or accept his authority? Paul's presentation here might help to remove the suspicion that Christians could not be good citizens.

Furthermore, many Christians were slaves. All the Christian talk about freedom might be considered inflammatory, a threat to the status quo, an inducement to the unrest natural among people living in bondage.

Paul's attitude to the state was conditioned by his view of reality. This world, and everything in it, is passing. Nothing that we experience here is permanent. 1 Corinthians 7 indicates that even the institution of marriage is transient. In that chapter, Christians are also told not to worry about whether they are free or slave, because earthly freedom and earthly slavery are without permanence. The important thing is that each person use his or her place in life as an opportunity to live as a new person in Christ.

At the same time, the state is a fact, as are marriage, work, one's place in life. Paul had earlier told the Thessalonians—

some of whom had stopped working because they believed that the world would end very soon—that they should go about their daily work. Believing that the institutions of this world are temporary does not mean "dropping out."

The institutions of the world as we know it are to be taken seriously. It is within them that one lives the Christian life. This is true while it is also true that the world as we know it will not last and will give way to the world as God intends it to be.

There is no ideal state. There is no state that has permanent, eternal existence. Every state, no matter how good, how sound, will end in dust. Empires and kingdoms have come and gone in the history of mankind. And so also will republics, democracies and any other models of government that might be forged.

No state or government or form of government ought to be canonized.

However, states can fulfill various functions that fit in with God's plans. They can provide the atmosphere and the opportunity for the service and love of neighbor. They can restrain the hatred and violence and injustice which are the result of sin in the world. They can provide peace and security in which men might face the significant issues of life and listen to the preaching of the Gospel as a key to interpreting those issues.

Reasons such as these are very likely behind Paul's insistence on obedience to authorities, on payment of taxes.

The Greek word translated as "obey" has a rather complex meaning. It can express the relationship of the Christian to God, of the Christian to leaders of the Church, of Christian wives and husbands to each other, of the Church to Christ, of Christ to the Father.

The general idea, broader than simple obedience, might be understood in this way.

There is a divinely appointed order to the relationships that exist between God and people, among people, between people and the universe they inhabit. All should observe the claims on their behavior that this order makes if God's plan is to come to fulfillment. Hence, there can be something very deeply Christian in observing a directive from a leader of the Church, or in obeying a law from a state official, or in living properly a husband-wife relationship.

This kind of belief prevents those who wield power from using it to exercise tyranny. Every relationship is subject to God's will. The Church leader must use his authority in accord with God's will, i.e., with charity and understanding and openness to the guidance of the Spirit.

The state must recognize that it too is subject to God's will and plan. When it makes demands or passes laws that come into conflict with what God has revealed and expects, it loses its God-given place in governing. When there is conflict between what the state demands and what Christ expects, for the Christian there should be no doubt that he should follow where Christ leads.

Paul is clearly affirming that the state has a place in the Christian scheme of things. At the same time, he would warn the state that it, too, is subject to God, that it is a transient reality. It loses its right to be obeyed when it comes into conflict with divinely revealed truths and with the dignity and rights that God has given to all men.

THE "WEAK" AND THE "STRONG" (Romans 14.1–15.13)

In First Corinthians, Paul had to face at some length this particular problem. It is the age-old problem of the misunderstanding possible between those who still feel themselves bound by certain observances if they are to live in a way pleasing to

God and those who feel that they can love and serve God without these observances. To use a familiar example, a good Catholic of twenty years ago would have felt that not eating meat on Friday was a rather significant part of the expression of his faith. Now we have been "liberated" from that observance. Suppose that some people still felt that not eating meat on Friday is fundamental to living out their faith? How should the meat-eaters and the non-meat-eaters come to terms with one another?

Paul raises this kind of question for his readers.

Paul probably does not have any specific information about Rome. However, his experience with different Christian communities taught him that there could be conflicts between those groups which kept ascetical practices, like abstaining from meat and wine (vv. 2, 17, 21) and those which did not. There was also a divergence of opinion on the special observance of certain days (v. 5), possibly for abstinence.

Paul's advice is the same here as in First Corinthians when he deals with the issue of eating meat that had been first offered to idols. The truly important matter is not whether one eats meat or does not eat meat, or whether one drinks wine or does not drink it. What counts is the effect that our actions have on others. Thus, the one who is convinced that eating or not eating meat makes no difference must be careful about what his example might do to someone whose conscience tells him that a Christian ought to abstain from meat at certain times.

Paul sums it up this way, "We who are strong in faith should be patient with the scruples of those whose faith is weak; we must not be selfish. Each should please his neighbor so as to do him good by building up his spirit" (15.1-2).

PERSONAL NOTES   (Romans 16)

The Letter to the Romans ends with a long list of greetings

and comments to individuals that Paul knew. For a number
of reasons, many modern scholars do not believe that this was
originally a part of the Letter to the Romans. For example, it
mentions by name a large number of individuals. This is very
unusual since Paul had not yet visited Rome. Where would he
have met and had contact with all these people if they were
now at Rome?

It is quite possible that this last chapter was originally addressed
to the Church at Ephesus where Paul had spent three years. At
some later time it was attached to the Letter to the Romans.
However, it also remains quite possible that it is in its proper
setting where it is now.

At any rate, the chapter reveals a side of Paul that is very personal. He expresses his love and appreciation for his friends
and fellow-workers.

A LOOK BACKWARD

As was indicated when we began the reading of this letter, it
deals most intensely with the meaning of Jesus Christ. Paul
has set himself to put into writing what he has been taught,
what his experience has shown him, what his own faith tells
him about the human situation.

The picture that emerges might seem negative and pessimistic.
And indeed it is—if the human has to stand by itself. By itself,
mankind is helplessly caught in the snare of sin. The past is
tainted by selfishness, hatred, injustice. There is no future
except a deeper plunge into sin and evil.

But the human race does not have to stand alone. It is never
without the love of God. That love is most obvious and most
active in the life, death and resurrection of Jesus Christ. This
rescues people from sin. It enables them to escape the accu-
mulated store of evil in the world. It places them in touch
with God himself. It offers the opportunity to get beyond
the evil and sin which are so obvious. It offers the opportunity

and strength to make God's love present, at least to some degree, here and now. It offers a future with God forever.

This is what Jesus meant to Paul.

The foremost issue for reflection for any of us who read the letter of Paul to the Romans is, "What does Jesus mean to me?"

SUGGESTIONS FOR REFLECTION

1. Sometimes people are shocked that Paul did not write against evils of his time like slavery, taxes, and other forms of oppression. Explain why he did not treat of these as evil in themselves; explain the attitude he recommended toward them.

2. What would be Paul's attitude toward modern styles of government, i.e., republics, democracies, dictatorships, etc.?

3. How does the government of your parish provide an atmosphere and opportunity for the service and love of neighbor?

4. What was Paul's attitude toward obedience to the state? Where does the state fit into God's plan for all men?

5. "What counts is the effect that our actions have on others." How might this operate in industry today? in our international and political relationships?

6. In speaking of a life with meaning, what would Paul advise? Look at your own life today and ask yourself honestly, "What does Jesus mean to me?" Share your answer with someone.

SUGGESTIONS FOR FURTHER READING

B. Ahern. *The Epistle to the Galatians and the Epistle to the Romans.* Collegeville: Liturgical Press, 1960.

The following are important, more advanced reference works containing commentaries on all the books of the Bible.

R. Brown, (ed.). *The Jerome Biblical Commentary.* Englewood Cliffs, N.J.: Prentice-Hall, 1968.

R. Fuller, (ed.). *A New Catholic Commentary on Holy Scripture.* London: Nelson, 1969.

C. Laymon, (ed.). *The Interpreter's One-Volume Commentary on the Bible.* Nashville: Abingdon Press, 1971.

For an over-all view of Pauline teaching on the college level:

G. Montague. *The Living Thought of St. Paul.* Milwaukee: Bruce, 1966.

Commentaries on Romans:

C. K. Barrett. *The Epistle to the Romans.* New York: Harper and Row, 1957.

E. Best. *The Letter of Paul to the Romans.* Cambridge: Cambridge University Press, 1967.

K. Schelkle. *The Epistle to the Romans: Theological Meditations.* New York: Herder and Herder, 1964.

Pauline Theology:

F. Amiot. *The Key Concepts of St. Paul.* New York: Herder and Herder, 1962.

L. Cerfaux. *The Spiritual Journey of St. Paul.* New York: Sheed and Ward, 1968.

H. Ridderbos. *Paul: An Outline of His Theology.* Grand Rapids: Eerdmans, 1975.

D. Whitely. *The Theology of St. Paul.* Philadelphia: Fortress, 1966.

Paul's life and missionary travels:

M. Muggeridge and A. Vidler. *Paul, Envoy Extraordinary.* New York: Harper and Row, 1972.